Keeping Your Dreams Alive

D0732404

Keeping Your Dreams Alive

Doug Murren

CREATION
HOUSE
BOOKS ABOUT SPIRIT-LED LIVING
ORLANDO, FLORIDA

Copyright © 1993 by Doug Murren
All rights reserved
Printed in the United States of America
Library of Congress Catalog Card Number: 92-74599
International Standard Book Number: 0-88419-279-2

Creation House
Strang Communications Company
190 North Westmonte Drive
Altamonte Springs, FL 32714
(407) 862-7565

This book or parts thereof may not be
reproduced in any form without prior written
permission of the publisher.

Unless otherwise noted, all Scripture quotations
are from the Holy Bible, New International Version.
Copyright © 1973, 1978, 1984, International
Bible Society. Used by permission.

*Dedicated to the memory of
Jamie Buckingham (1932-1992),
my friend and mentor whom I miss greatly,
and to his wife, Jackie, who continues to
encourage so many. Thank you!*

CONTENTS

PREFACE

So who needs a book about a dreamer? You!

That is, if you want to leave a mark on this earth and fill a void only you can fill.

You may be a student just beginning to invest in your dream. You will need to know what to do when your coat gets stolen.

Or maybe you are a businessperson starting on a new venture, or you have just had a sudden career change at mid-life. You, too, will want to know how to keep your dreams alive.

You may even be a pastor — with or without a church — who doesn't want to dream anymore.

Or you may be a mother who sees great promise as a

gifted woman guiding a home — yet you yearn for personal fulfillment for your own unspoken dreams.

Perhaps you are a retired person. Your working days are through, but you've got a lot of dreaming left to do.

This book is for all adventurers who can't see letting an entire life pass by without a dream coming true.

JOSEPH THE DREAMER

Joseph is a fruitful vine,
    a fruitful vine near a spring,
    whose branches climb over a wall.
With bitterness archers attacked him;
    they shot at him with hostility.
But his bow remained steady,
    his strong arms stayed limber,
because of the hand of the Mighty One of Jacob,
    because of the Shepherd, the Rock of Israel,
because of your father's God, who helps you,
    because of the Almighty, who blesses you
with blessings of the heavens above,
    blessings of the deep that lies below,
    blessings of the breast and womb.
Your father's blessings are greater
    than the blessings of the ancient mountains,
    than the bounty of the age-old hills.
Let all these rest on the head of Joseph,
    on the brow of the prince among his brothers.

Genesis 49:22-26

INTRODUCTION

I am not qualified to write a book about dreams. But I have never met anyone else who was either.

So, being an adventurer, I decided to sit down and study Joseph's life with you. This massive section of the book of Genesis (chapters 37-50) sets the stage for understanding how God lays the groundwork for Joseph's dreaming. It will help you to turn to the back of the book to appendix A and look at a brief overview of Joseph's life.

The great dreamer Joseph fascinates me. I'll confess to you that some of his supernatural experiences set me a little on edge. However, once I read the story through fifty or sixty times, I concluded that it wasn't so bad.

It isn't often in the Bible you get to look into someone

else's life for nearly one hundred years. We are introduced to Joseph at age 17, see a surprising turn at age 30 and follow him in his old age up to 110 years.

Joseph is a paradigm for Christians today. Why? Well, let's take a look at him and his surroundings. He lived in a time when scarcity faced the world. (Sounds familiar, doesn't it?) He was also a hard-to-handle, spoiled adolescent. (He would fit in perfectly with the culture of American adolescents.) He was skillful in moving through supernatural realms. (With the emergence of the New Age movement, our culture is clearly becoming more and more comfortable with the supernatural. The advent of the Pentecostal and charismatic movements could easily earmark our century as one of the most supernatural in church history.)

He was the victim of a dysfunctional family (a standard in our society). A dysfunctional family is a family that doesn't work the way it is supposed to. In Joseph's case it was a dysfunctional, blended family. His father happened to be a guy named Jacob, but everyone called him Tricky Jake because of the way he stole the birthright from his older brother, Esau. Tricky Jake had two wives, two concubines and a house full of kids who were all messed up (see appendix B for helpful chart illustrating this complex family).

WHAT'S A PARADIGM?

A paradigm is a model or a way of seeing reality. I like to think of it as a pattern you can sketch around. A paradigm does three things:

1. It defines success.

2. It sets the boundaries of behavior.

3. It tells us the rules of the game we are playing.

When my wife used to make clothes for our kids in our early marriage, she would start by buying rolls of fabric and a pattern. While I studied my college textbooks, I would watch out of the corner of my eye, fascinated, as she laid out the pattern and pinned it to the fabric. To me, the pattern looked like a bunch of unrelated shapes of limp paper.

Our lives are shaped by contact with the Bible in the same way. We lay down the fabric of our lives, place the pattern of biblical figures on top of it and see how we line up. Then God starts the cutting. Another word for pattern is *template*, which Webster defines as a "metal, wooden or paper plate for forming an accurate copy of an object or shape." Many commentators say that Joseph's life was cut from the template of Christ. Joseph reflected how the servant Christ laid down His life to establish a spiritual home for His church.

In Joseph's life we see:

- definitions of true success;

- the boundaries within which dreamers are called to work; and

- some rules by which authentic dreamers live.

We are invited to identify with the template of biblical figures whose life stories are told in Scripture. The patriarch Joseph shows us all the twists and turns dreamers must go through. He gives us courage to face the unexpected as he did. His story gives us hope when we face the confused days, delays, disappointments and fears that attach themselves to our dreams.

We will grasp, as Joseph did, that God loves the dream receiver much more than any dream He gives. We will see that all dreams must be tested and cultivated before the fulfillment arrives. Finally, we will learn how we can keep our dreams — even when they steal our coats.

LET'S GET MORE ACQUAINTED WITH A DREAMER

The name Joseph means "God will add" (see Gen. 30:24).

God chooses names carefully. Joseph was going to *add* a great deal to God's plan. He was going to be the person who would help move the people of God into a whole new history and fulfilled promise — to return to the land of Canaan and conquer it.

You have a special name, too, a name that is descriptive of God's plan for you. A friend told me that my name, Doug, means "he who dwells in a dark forest." That's not the most inspiring meaning, is it? But another person handed me a plaque that said the name means "seeker of truth." That sounded much better. However, no matter what my present name means, God has a name for me that matches His work in my life (see Rev. 2:17). This name is known only to us and to God.

Back to Joseph, this guy that God is going to "add" through. Joseph's name itself implies he would see good things happen wherever he went. But things usually work in reverse with God's heavenly logic. God subtracts to add — just as He loses to gain, dies to live, gives to receive and serves to rule.

We will see that Joseph's life was filled with complexities. He often changed roles just as he was getting the part down right. You and I have multiple roles, just as Joseph did. In his life Joseph became:

- a brother and a half brother. Joseph's only full brother was Benjamin, but he also had ten half brothers.

- his father's favorite son. He was the firstborn son of Jacob's favorite wife, Rachel.

- a regular visitor to the tailor. Jacob kept his favorite son busy with fittings for a richly or-

14

namented robe.

- a hated brother. His brothers knew he was favored — and they hated him for it.

- a dreamer of dreams. He dreamed that his father, mother and brothers were bowing down to him.

- a guy who evidently had difficulty getting a good night's sleep.

- a seventeen-year-old smart aleck. He shared his dream brashly with his family, who did not receive it too warmly.

- an apprentice shepherd. Joseph tended the flocks with his brothers, endearing himself to them by advising their father whenever they did something wrong.

- a slave. At first his brothers plotted to kill him, but the eldest finally convinced them to sell Joseph to a Midianite slave trader.

- a consummate manager — faithful, trustworthy and honest. Joseph became the manager of his Egyptian master's household, and all he did was blessed.

- the object of lust. The wife of his master, Potiphar, found Joseph to be attractive and frequently propositioned him, much to his dismay.

- a guy in prison for sexual harrassment. Potiphar's wife accused Joseph falsely of attacking her.

- a forgotten friend. Joseph correctly interpreted a dream for one of his fellow inmates, who was released but forgot about Joseph.

- a well-kept secret of God in Egypt. While Joseph's life seemed to have gone from bad to worse, God was preparing to use him to save his family — and the whole earth — from starvation.

- a prison trustee. The warden of the prison put Joseph in charge of all prison operations.

- an ex-convict. Joseph was released from prison after interpreting Pharaoh's dream.

- a consummate ruler. Pharaoh put Joseph in charge of the whole land of Egypt to prepare for the famine the dream predicted.

- a father. Pharaoh gave Joseph a wife, who bore him two sons.

- an international political strategist. He was able to parlay Pharaoh's food supply into international economic power.

- an international businessman and economist. In the years of famine, Joseph sold grain to all nations of the earth.

- a symbol of a Savior to come. Joseph's redemptive suffering pointed toward a coming Messiah.

Joseph's story demonstrates that dreamers are a motley crew indeed.

As God surveys His people, He must feel like the Duke of Wellington before the Battle of Waterloo. While surveying his troops prepared for battle, the Iron Duke exclaimed, "I don't know if they'll scare the enemy, but, by God, they frighten me."

The beauty of God's plan is that He can start with a cocky 17-year-old and end up with a 110-year-old savior.

Even though God's plan for Joseph's life culminated in

highest honor, the process was not nearly as glorious. Joseph's name meant "God will add," but a lot was subtracted from his life before anything was added. The same is true for us: If we are true dreamers of God, we will lose as much as we will gain.

Exhibit number one is Joseph's coat. Joseph's coat would have been highly embellished and long enough to reach to the wrists and ankles. It was a nobleman's or king's coat, which primarily stood as a sign of his inheritance. It said, "This kid gets it all." It spurred in his brothers the fear that there wasn't enough to go around. Joseph wore it proudly, arrogantly and stupidly. He didn't realize that he didn't have a dream — a dream was about to have him.

LIFE APPLICATION

Here is a little exercise for you before we begin to follow Joseph's life journey. After seeing some of the roles Joseph played, look at some of the roles you are playing now. Then compare them to your dream for the future.

Outline some of the titles and positions you have in life.

What is your dream, or do you have one?

Who will you be when you are through dreaming? (This may be a key to enjoying the in-between.)

What name do you think God would call you if you were to get your secret name now?

I found the above exercise quite stretching for me. After all, which of us has ever really gone all the way on our journey without a little fear or hesitancy to take a good look at ourselves? That is what a good dream does. It makes the dreamers look at themselves. Before his dreaming was finished, Joseph did, and so will you and I.

Let us now move on to learn how a God-given dream owns you as you grow. We will also see that it's not the dream that makes the difference, but the One we are traveling with as the dream unfolds.

ONE

JOSEPH
THE DREAMER

Joseph had a dream (Gen. 37:5).

So you want to be a dreamer? Let's see what a dream is. The word could describe several kinds of experiences.

- A dramatic scene or event seen in the imagination during sleep.

- A plan for your life. The term can by used synonymously with the word *vision*.

- An event or scene generated by God's Spirit, often interpreted by others. (This can come as a vision when one is awake.)

- A hopeful expectation about how our future can be better.

Rather than keying in on one of these experiences of dreaming, we will journey on the pathway to understanding what it means to be a dreamer. I've concluded all of the above merge together in the heart of a dreamer.

How we receive our dream is secondary to who we are as dreamers. Whether our dreams come when we are awake or asleep is not important. Though we receive dreams in many different ways, the character and journey of dreamers tend to have many commonalities. Joseph, as we've established, is the ideal template of a dreamer.

CAN I WIN?

You probably want to be a successful dreamer or you wouldn't have picked up this book. Well, the kind of success we are going to find in Joseph's story may surprise you. After all, we all have our own definitions of success, even if we haven't thought it through and written it down. And our definition of success will shape the quality of our dreams.

When I was in high school, a hot car was the ultimate definition of success. Later on, having the latest Fender, "Strat" or Gibson guitar and giant "amps" defined success for the musical type. For a while in college, having the best drugs seemed to bring some a higher level of status.

Then I got involved in church stuff, and the rules changed. On top of that, they have changed several times since then. I had finally given up learning how to keep score for spiritual stuff. Then I became a preacher and found that "success" was measurable — it was Sunday morning attendance. For a businessperson, dollars in the till may define success. Or a mid-life wife might define success as meaningful work. These are all OK. After all, reaching people for Christ does mean there will be more people to listen to you preach. And conducting a business without profit wouldn't be considered a satisfactory way to go through life, would it? Last, it can be healthy for a wife to find meaningful work outside the home.

Our definition of success will also shape our real values. Values are what you bring to the dreams that make them work. They fuel it. They drive it. Jesus' message illustrates a value-driven dream. He values us because we are created in His image, and He gave His life to restore us.

Joseph pummels us with a pattern of biblical success that extracts the best from life. His experience signals all dreamers to stop and define success before dreaming. We are to pause, beware, take note and, as Christ said, "estimate the cost" before we move on (see Luke 14:25-33).

Joseph shows us that success isn't something you achieve; it is something you already recognize around you. We all have it. Or, better yet, when we look at life from God's perspective, we see it in the simplicity of being formed in His image.

Before we move on, let's fill out another little questionnaire here. Be honest! It will help you later on. Answer one of the following questions.

I would feel good about myself if I could:

1.

2.

3.

4.

At my funeral I want my four best friends to say:

1.

2.

3.

4.

I guess my parents will call me a success when:

1.

2.

3.

4.

I think what is really important to God in my life right now is:

1.

2.

3.

4.

Were you honest? I hope so. Your answers could begin to help you discover what your dream is and how you will define success.

ASKING THE RIGHT QUESTIONS

Paul told Timothy that all Scripture is useful for teaching, rebuking, correcting and training in righteousness, so that the man of God may be thoroughly equipped for good work (see 2 Tim. 3:16-17). Of course, Paul was talking about the Old Testament. So that means we can learn a lot from Joseph. The question is how to go about it.

Understanding Scripture entails two very important processes:

- Asking the right questions.

- Identifying with every aspect of the biblical characters studied so you learn all you can about yourself.

Have you ever wondered about questions like these: Why did Christ come as a baby? Why didn't He come with armies and nuclear weapons? Why all alone and vulnerable as a baby in a manger? If you think about these questions, you will come up with an answer, maybe several. One answer I came up with was this: He came as a baby to show us God's disdain for power. A simple birth illustrated once and for all that the enemy wasn't really so tough.

I think that coming as a baby in a manger was ultimately a joke on hell. You see, I believe God is a trickster. God's logic was to overcome terrible, rebellious evil with a plan that started with a baby's whimper and ended with the cry, "Father, forgive them!" Never forget God's logic: You lose to gain; you give to receive; you die to live.

Let's ask some questions about Joseph. Why did young Joseph have to go through so much turmoil just to get his family to move down south? What pleased God about his character?

I believe Joseph's struggles show us that *no dream just happens*. Reality sometimes gets worse before it starts to line up with the dream.

Joseph's character demonstrates that in serving we find our greatest success. We see him first serving his father by taking messages to his brothers in the fields. Then we see him boldly serving Potiphar. When he was in prison, Joseph served the warden as the highest trustee. Finally, he served Pharaoh as the ruler of the land. The message is clear: The way up is down, as Dante's famous saying goes.

TWO

THE KID WHO
LOST HIS COAT

Then they got Joseph's robe, slaughtered a goat and dipped the robe in the blood. They took the ornamented robe back to their father (Gen. 37:31-32).

He left his cloak in her hand and ran out of the house (Gen. 39:12).

Have you ever lost a coat? I recently lost a coat for the first time, but then I found it again. My brother Todd, however, hasn't been so fortunate. In fact, his loss may be the reason I cling tightly to every coat I get.

I remember well his coatless return home. It wasn't

pretty. Mom looked at him, as only redheaded moms can, and asked, "How do you lose a winter coat at school?"

Todd shrugged his shoulders with no reply, and tears welled up in his eyes. It seems there was no reasonable explanation as to how a kid could lose a coat on a winter day in central Washington when the weather was twenty degrees. I decided it must have been easier than it looked. Todd was a smart fellow, and I determined thereafter to work hard to make certain that I never lost a coat.

When I took my coat off at the playground, I watched it closely, sometimes placing a rock on it. I knew I didn't want a lecture like the one my brother had received: "Do you think we're made of money? We can't buy you a coat every week!"

If I remember correctly, Todd lost another coat a few years later. Fate must have been playing a dirty trick on him.

The coat I lost recently belonged originally to my grandfather. When my grandfather died twelve years ago, I inherited his beautiful, gray plaid, Filson hunting jacket. I loved that coat. It reminded me of my grandfather. Some of the pockets still smelled like the Beeman gum he used to give me when I was ten years old. Even as a forty-year-old I received great comfort from that coat.

How excited I was when my friend Mike called and said he had found my coat in his closet (though I was perturbed that he had waited several months to tell me). I had been calling members of the congregation and accusing them of stealing my coat. I am wearing it again this winter, beating back the Seattle cold with this wonderful woolen heirloom passed on to me by my loving grandfather.

Joseph lost two coats in his lifetime (that we know of). The first was taken when his brothers sold him into slavery. The other was lost at the hands of a would-be seducer. It looks to me as if God didn't mind at all that Joe lost two coats. You can be certain he isn't the only dreamer God has stripped to his skivvies.

If you are a dreamer, God has a test for you. It will be bigger than you, and it will probably involve being de-coated along the way. One of the subplots we discover in Joseph's story is that it is a painful process to realize that the coat isn't what contains the dream. The coat may be a good thing, but it is not the dream God wants for your life. We wear coats in the form of titles, possessions or status — things that make us feel important. God's dreams always entail a stripping away to levels no one can see — the place where dreams of value reside.

GOD'S DREAMS HAVE US

As I look at Joseph's story, I am convinced that none of us really has a dream, but God's dreams have us. None of us can cling to our coats saying, "Look at this. This is God's dream for me. I'm going to hold on to it with all my might." God's dreams are bigger than the coats we find to symbolize them.

I remember an opportunity I had in college to make my debut in the singing ministry.

On the way home from church one day, the assistant pastor grabbed my arm and said, "Doug, you are doing a fine job in the youth department as a volunteer. We are looking for someone who could be strong in music too. Would you like a chance to sing the special on a Sunday next month?"

Now this wasn't any small, backwoods church. We were attending a big city church while we were in college. Several hundred people were in attendance. The Holy Spirit was moving powerfully. It was a big deal to be asked to sing.

I was ecstatic on the way home. I turned to Deb (now my wife) and said, "I believe God is about to open new vistas of opportunity in ministry for me." Smirking, she replied, "Can't wait to see." I have since seen that smirk many times throughout our marriage. Now I tremble whenever it appears.

That week I went to the music store and picked out the music. I enthusiastically returned the next week for our first rehearsal. I sang the Andrae Crouch song beautifully in rehearsal. I even mastered the African-American intricacies of his style. It was going to be great! (My ministry was expanding, and I knew it, and it was all happening when I was just a junior in college!)

Finally the fateful weekend came. On the way to the church I somehow felt in my stomach that it wasn't going to be good. I don't know how we know such things. Maybe the Holy Spirit gives us warnings like *"Red alert!* You are about to be creamed for the sake of your own spiritual growth."

On that morning we practiced the song again, reading the music over the shoulder of the assistant pastor, who was accompanying me. The refrain had a particularly high range to it. He warned me not to get into the wrong octave lest we both suffer embarrassment.

Sitting in the service that morning, I began to sweat. I knew my number had been called. You know the number — the one they have in heaven. I could almost hear the angels talking:

"Number 113 is up."

"Who's that?"

"Oh, that's the redhead. He's ready for Stealing Your Coat, lesson number one."

I was relieved when we went past the section of the service when the special music was usually sung. The sermon that followed was terrific. We progressed on through the morning, and then at the end of the service, quite out of the ordinary, the pastor said, "This morning we are going to end with a special song by a strong young man in the Lord, Doug Murren. Doug, come and sing for us."

As I started toward the podium, the assistant pastor reached out and tried to take the music from me. It was the only sheet of music I had for the lyrics. There we were, at the front of the church, pulling the music back and forth. Finally he whispered aggressively, "This is the only sheet of music we have, and I can't play without it. Well, do the best you can, Doug, and we'll see how it goes."

Frightened, I responded, "But I don't know the words without the music." How I wished I had memorized the thing. I thought, Easy for you to stay calm since you are down in the music pit where they can't see you, and I am standing three feet above everyone where they can look straight into my scared eyes.

As we entered into the first verse, I forgot the lyrics. I was so rattled that I just hummed the melody. There I was, "Hmm hmm hummm humm." I could hear scattered laughing throughout the congregation, but I pressed on anyway.

The assistant pastor looked up from the piano only for a millisecond, then he lowered his head and played on even more intently. I was alone.

I could feel my splendid coat slipping off. Eventually we came to the refrain (remember the warning about getting into the wrong octave?). You guessed it. I did. We proceeded into ranges that even sopranos trained for decades can't reach. I did the only thing I knew to do, and that was to hit wrong notes all the way down the scale, trying to get to the right key.

At this point I watched the pastor fall over sideways in the front pew into his wife's lap, laughing hysterically. Then laughter and clapping broke out throughout the congregation as the assistant pastor played on.

Finally the song came to an end. The song was so wonderfully titled *He Looked Beyond My Faults and Saw My Needs*.

I was shattered. I decided that I wouldn't return to the

church if I had anything to say about it. But the Lord had the final word, and I did return the next week without my coat. My dream was still intact, but I was a great deal humbler.

So what is the first lesson a dreamer learns? Know the difference between your dream and your coat. Your dream is a permanent calling from God that requires a process of cultivation for fulfillment. Your coat — whatever gives you a feeling of status — is a temporary symbol that God may choose to take away. God is more interested in who the dream makes you than what the dream is.

Losing your coat doesn't mean losing your dream.

THREE

YOUR LIFE IS
A SYMPHONY

They stripped him of his robe (Gen. 37:23).

[Joseph] lived in the house of his Egyptian master (Gen. 39:2).

Joseph's master took him and put him in prison (Gen. 39:20).

So Pharaoh said to Joseph, "I hereby put you in charge of the whole land of Egypt" (Gen. 41:41).

If Joseph focused on losing his coat, he might have despaired of ever seeing the fulfillment to his dream.

However, when we look at his life as a whole, we see that the coat incident was just a single movement in a much greater symphony.

Our lives progress in movements as well. If you are younger, you probably see some of the minor themes as major movements, but you'll see the major movements as you grow older. Most of my friends are now in mid-life and hitting some of the later movements in their lives. It's a major shock to them. They thought all of life would be like adolescence.

In Joseph's life we see at least four movements.

MOVEMENT 1: UNREFINED DREAMER

What else can you call a smart-aleck seventeen-year-old with such high-caliber dreams from God? After all, he had a dream that all his brothers, his mother and his father would bow to him. And then he had no tact about it. He just went and blurted out the whole thing at the breakfast table. I have found that most dreamers share this deficiency in tact, especially if they have achieved a little success. A little adversity here and there will help any dreamer.

MOVEMENT 2: UNDAUNTED SLAVE

You have to hand it to Joseph — he made the best of a bad situation. All dreamers need a supply of his kind of resilience. One of my doctor friends explained to me that emotional resilience really has to do with the amount of serotonin the body produces. People with more serotonin bounce back more quickly than those with low amounts. It looks like Joe had a great ability to produce serotonin because he kept bouncing back over and over again.

The kid gained character quickly, too, and not from the example of his parents, Jacob and Rachel. Tricky Jake cheated his older brother, Esau, to get the firstborn's birthright and blessing. When Rachel learned that Jacob was moving their family from her hometown, she stole her father's household gods and hid them under her skirts when her tent was searched.

Joseph, in contrast, rolled up his sleeves and went the way of character, faithfulness and integrity. The evidence here says that adversity does make for greatness.

OK, so you might settle for mediocrity once in a while after you read the story. But just think what you'll miss if you take that route.

MOVEMENT 3: INNOCENT SUFFERER

Boy, I hate being accused of something I didn't do. But how about this: Joseph served prison time for sexual harassment when he was entirely guilt-free. In fact, *he* was the one being harassed! Worse yet — the woman was his boss's wife. As a young man, Joseph showed great character in resisting temptation and enduring the false accusation. The lesson for dreamers is that one test may just be getting you ready for another test.

MOVEMENT 4: FORGIVING SAVIOR

In the final movement of his life, at 110 years old, Joseph stands as a symbol of our great Savior, Jesus. Joseph had saved his clan, and the entire world, from starvation by organizing food storage in Egypt. He had controlled the commodities market of the whole world and made Pharaoh incredibly wealthy. He had suffered so that others could prosper.

He knew from experience that God's destiny is everything. He shows us, too, that when you let one of God's dreams own you, the reward will come — though it may take a lifetime.

HOW ABOUT YOU?

Can you see the movements in your life developing? Recognizing movements will give you more appreciation for what God is doing. At the age of forty-one I can see that possibly all four of the movements of Joseph's life have cycled through my life in some measure.

Our spiritual lives have an ebb and flow to them. Movements come in and go out. Sometimes they are loud; sometimes they are soft. A life lived in God's dreams is like Beethoven's Fifth Symphony: *ba ba ba baaaaa* reappears again and again in different forms.

I am intrigued with Joseph's ability to be comfortable in whatever state he found himself. It seemed as if he were simply drifting through a great symphony, enjoying each new change of instrumentation and tempo, the occasional crash of cymbals and the glissando of the violins. In all of it he heard one thing: the plan of God.

I have looked back over the great dreamers I have known. One who comes to mind is Frank Kline, one of my college professors. He developed and purchased patents in America and gave them to poor Christians in Asia and India for a small fee. The patents gave those Christians a way to finance ministries in their countries for decades to come.

When I knew Dr. Kline, he was in his retirement years. It was obviously a whole new movement for him and frustrating in some respects. His days of adventure and risk were behind him, but now he was sharing with his students what it was like to be a dreamer.

I also remember getting to know Edwin Orr, the world's foremost authority on revivals. I remember one afternoon in particular, while having dinner in our home, he told me about Evan Roberts, the leader of the great Welsh Revival in 1906. He himself had been part of the Bethel Band that helped evangelize China at the time Watchman Nee was building his churches. Orr also had a symphony in his life with recognizable movements. If I had known then what I know now, I would have learned a lot more from him. And I would have been more prepared for the changing movements in my own life.

Both of my children are getting ready to leave home now, a big change for all of us. Though a movement is ending, my dream is still the same. I plan to spend my life pastoring in Seattle, Washington, the most unchurched city in America. And at the end of my life I want to be able to say that Seattle is, in some measure, more spiritually healthy than when I started.

When God's dreams have us, it helps to look forward to the culmination of the dream and then work backward (a concept we'll discuss more in chapter 15). Through all the painful movements of his life, Joseph looked forward to the culmination of his dream: One day he would see his family again, and they would bow down before him. The changing movements just brought his dream closer to reality.

Interestingly, all the movements in Joseph's life had a common theme: service. God often asks us to serve other people's dreams before our dreams are fully accomplished.

Most pastors who lead large churches were themselves on the pastoral staff of other large churches. I myself served nine years on the staff of a church and was committed to serving a group of people whom I loved a great deal. Now that I have my own congregation, I have committed myself to serve for their success. I am mentoring my own group of pastors as well, and I hope to see them succeed with their own congregations. I believe all great dreams are fulfilled by helping others to be successful.

As we've seen, great dreamers know how to go to the end of their lives and work backward. As the psalmist wrote, "Teach us to number our days aright, that we may gain a heart of wisdom" (Ps. 90:12). Dreamers "live by faith, not by sight" (2 Cor. 5:7).

In some cases we may not even fully understand the extent of the dream until the final movement of our lives. For example, when he was young, Joseph recognized the dream that his family would honor him, but just before his death he realized God had a larger purpose of preparing a people to return to the land of Canaan and conquer it (see Gen. 50:24-25). That's why he asked his sons to carry his bones with them when they went to the land of promise.

Though we may recognize part of our dream now, we need to trust the Dream Giver. He'll keep us on the path to *His* dreams for us.

FOUR

DOES GOD STILL SPEAK THROUGH DREAMS?

Then Joseph said to them, "Do not interpretations belong to God? Tell me your dreams" (Gen. 40:8).

SCENE: *Pharaoh's palace, 1625 B.C., administrative wing by a water pool, overlooking a window.*

JOSEPH: I am an old man now, in my nineties. I still dream occasionally. I was seventeen when I had my first important dream. I remember it well. It wasn't like the other dreams I had. Most of my dreams were fueled by fears and the normal musings of an adolescent mind charged by hormones.

But when I had that dream, I thought I had to tell everyone. If only I could live those moments over. I remember the smell of the Bedouin tent as I hurried in that morning. All eleven of my brothers were around the table, with my father and all his concubines and wives. I blurted out, "I've had a dream; I've had a dream! Listen to my dream."

My father placed me on the chair of honor and gave me a box of camel skin pillows so that I could sit higher than my brothers. As I peered down into their eyes, I said, "We were all binding sheaves of grain out in the field. Suddenly my sheaf rose and stood upright, while all of your sheaves gathered around it and bowed down to it."

No one said a word.

Then there was the second dream. I announced again that I had had a dream, and my father was pleased. He seemed to enjoy the tension that rose in my brothers' hearts over my blessing.

I know it had something to do with my looking like my mother, Rachel. I would often hear him tell the servants that I had her intelligence and spiritual sensitivities.

Once again I sat on the pillows, this time with my robe dangling around my ankles, reminding them all that I would be the chief inheritor. I spoke quickly and insensitively: "This time the sun and moon and eleven stars were bowing down to me." My father understood at once that my dream meant he, too, would be bowing down to me.

"Joseph, what is this dream you have had?" he said. "Do you think that your mother and I will bow down to you also?"

Though my brothers were jealous, I could tell that my father kept the matter deeply in mind. I still remember the lines around his eyes, the twist of his mouth. It was the face of one who was not fooled easily.

Dreams and interpreting dreams — they have been my life. If I could have only known the meaning of it before it began.... But God has been with me every step of the way. A dreamer I am! By dreams I have been made.

SCENE: *Home, A.D. 1975, 240 Lowe Street, bedroom with Bibles spread on bed.*

ME: I haven't slept well for days. There has been great conflict in the leadership of our church. The numbers aren't adding up in the accounting department. I fear the pastor or the business administrator is being taken advantage of. I just can't figure out which one.

The dream started coming after I prayed and fasted for two or three days. I would see pictures of me and my family floating in the air and moving away. Then a voice would say, "Move or be destroyed." As a member of a charismatic church, I assume the supernatural is a part of life. But this has never happened to me before. I don't know what will happen if I stay at this church, but I do know that this dream is supernatural.

I once heard it said that no one can tell where roads not taken might have led. I know that God is speaking to me through the urgent warning, "Move or be destroyed."

It also sounds like an indictment on those around me, but I don't have the stomach for sharing that.

I shared the dream with few people over the years. I did share it with my spiritual compatriot and good friend, the late Jamie Buckingham. (Jamie was well known as an author, columnist and speaker.) Some twenty years my senior, I felt he would understand it. He did.

It wasn't a dream of success, and I certainly didn't feel the promise of safety. But I felt a great deal of peace in obeying it.

It is now eighteen years later, and I lead a wonderful church. I know now that the church I left had a scandal that would have in fact destroyed me. You see, the business administrator had embezzled almost $600,000. The pastor had innocently been led into some mismanagement that set everyone up to look bad. I see now that I probably never would have been able to move and start a congregation in Seattle without God's message in the middle of the night.

I haven't learned how to ask God to give a dream, but I firmly believe that He still uses dreams to speak to us under certain conditions.

LEAVE ME ALONE — I WANT TO SLEEP

Dealing with dreams is a delicate matter. I have learned to be shy about sharing my dreams. I remember hearing a friend of mine tell a psychologist about his dream of soaring through the clouds and looking for someone. The psychologist responded: "Well, that's a sexual dream."

My friend was startled. I was interested in what the psychologist would say next.

"Oh, yes. Anytime you are flying in your dreams, it's an expression of sexual frustration."

That did it for me. I wasn't about to share any of my dreams.

I did have a recurring dream over a number of years about pastoring two churches. One church was in my hometown, and the other was in Seattle, where I pastor now. I would actually wake up in a cold sweat worrying I was at the wrong church. I bet I had this dream ten to fifteen times. Don't write me about the interpretation! The dream has stopped, and I'm glad! It's a terrible feeling to wake up during your dream (if you know that feeling, you know what I mean) and find out you're preaching in the wrong pulpit. You're supposed to be in Seattle, but you're in central Washington.

Actually, I think the dream stopped when I finally settled the fact that it wasn't my church; it was His church. Perhaps in my own subconsciousness the Holy Spirit was trying to get me to take my hands off and let loose a little bit. I've done that to some extent. Through prayer with friends and some counseling, I realized I probably was a little too enmeshed with our church. At any rate, the dream ceased.

My experiences have caused me to conclude there are several kinds of dreams (of the bedtime variety):

- The musings of a traumatized or fearful mind, warning that all is not well inwardly. This requires the special skill of counselors at times. Perhaps, for the most part, the dream is best left alone.

- The what-did-I-eat-last-night variety. These are the kind where an excessive amount of the chemical tryptophan feeds dream mechanisms in your brain which rehearse over and over again something that particularly caught your mind during the day (which has nothing to do with food, by the way).

- God-given dreams. This is the kind Joseph
  had, the rarest of all dreams.

A dream can be technically defined as imaginal, sen-
sory, motor and thought processes occurring during sleep.
Most authorities believe, however, that neither sleeping
nor dreaming can be defined precisely.

Dreaming usually takes place, in varying degrees, in
all stages of sleep. A dream usually involves visual im-
agery combined with sound and touch. We all have approximately five dreams per night, and most humans will
have somewhere around 136,000 dreams in a lifetime. We
spend the equivalent of six years dreaming.[1]

So we are all dreamers in a sense. Psychologists have
also found that there seems to be a biological and emotional need for REM (rapid eye movement) sleep, which is
when most dreaming occurs. In short, we all need to
dream to stay healthy.

Many scholars and even Christian counselors believe
that dreams should be stimulated, recorded and used as
helpful guides in our lives. That sounds dangerous to me.
If we have a total of 136,000 dreams in our lifetime, and
a guy like Joseph, who is an above-average dreamer, records two as being authentically motivated by the Lord,
I'm not sure I want to increase my God-inspired dreaming. Maybe we're supposed to let dreams just come as
they may.

Dreaming has often been a subject of controversy. An
Egyptian papyrus dating back to about the time of
Joseph had a great deal of discussion about dreams and
their interpretation. In ancient Greece a dreamer was
believed to be inspired by the gods. For example, in
Homer's *Iliad* (800 B.C.) dreams were considered messages from the gods.

We modern Westerners, however, want to escape the
fact that the Bible says God can and does communicate to
us through our dreams. This is an obvious statement to

people from Eastern cultures.

However, dreams shouldn't be seen as God's primary way of guiding us. I believe a dream may be God's way of getting our attention at a critical time or perhaps His communique of last resort.

Let's say it would be realistic for us to believe that we would have one, two, three — perhaps more — God-inspired dreams in our lifetime. What should we do with them when we have them? For me, I think dreams ought to be treated in the spirit of 1 Corinthians 14 — not with skepticism or with gullibility, but with clear evaluation.

THE SEEDS OF GOD'S PURPOSES

I think the aging Joseph, whose mind we entered earlier in this chapter, would view his dream of the sheaves, the sun, the moon and the stars as seeds — seeds that were planted in his heart. Our dreams can also be seeds of what lies ahead.

As I was growing up, I gardened with my grandfather. He was my best friend. Every summer we would plant a garden of about one and a half acres in size. First we would plow the field and rake up the weeds until there wasn't even a sign of unwanted vegetation. Then we'd smooth out the soil with a small tractor.

Next came the making of furrows. My grandfather had a human-driven plow that could dig a furrow an inch to three inches deep. My job was to plow the furrows as straight as possible. My grandfather taught me to run string between two stakes and plow along that line for approximately one hundred feet, making furrows that were one to one and a half inches deep. Next I took carrot or beet seeds and spread them evenly along the holes. Then we would go back through with the plow again, covering the seeds with an inch or less of dirt.

Then we would make mounds for squash and, of course, potatoes. In preparation my grandfather had purchased many bags of potatoes weeks earlier. We would cut out the worm-like "eyes" and plant them in well-prepared mounds of manure and dirt.

The greatest difficulty my grandfather had with me was teaching the principle of farmer's patience. It bothered me that weeks would go by, and I couldn't see what was happening under the ground. It got even worse when the carrots began to pop their little green heads up through the dirt. The thought of what was happening underground was too tempting. So when my grandfather would go to town to pick up some things he needed for work around the house, I would ask to stay home. Sneaking out into the field, I would pull up sections of carrots to see how the little buggers were doing.

There was one problem. Weeks later, the ones I had checked on could be spotted by their dwarfed size.

Dreams and revelations work this way. Because they are seeds of what will occur in the future, they need to be left in the ground and allowed to grow. This was what occurred in Joseph's life. As an old man, I think he recognized this. God planted a seed, and it took a lifetime to grow. How many of us have the patience to leave the seed in the ground without pulling it up periodically to check it out?

I have had a few dreams that I won't tell you about in this book. I'm not going to pull them up. I want to let them grow. Some of my dreams may never appear in my time, just as the cloud of witnesses in Hebrews 11 was "commended for their faith, yet none of them received what had been promised (v. 39).

I think God is like my grandfather. I can remember my grandfather saying, "Doug, you'll never make a farmer if you aren't patient enough to leave the seed in the ground."

I think God says to all of us, "You'll never be a dreamer unless you can leave the dream in the ground long enough to let it grow."

TESTING A DREAM

If we are going to nurture a dream seed in our hearts, we need to take steps to make sure it is authentically from God. The following is a checklist to help test the validity of supernatural manifestations, including dreams.

- Has experiencing the spiritual gift or manifestation taken your will from you? If so, it is not from God (1 Cor. 14:32). God will never overcome your personality. He will never force you to do things against your will. Rather He will invite and inspire. He wants to be a partner with you. Your dream or vision should make you more authentically you. It shouldn't seem unnatural for you.

- Is it peaceful? Is this phenomenon palatable and intelligible to other people? If not, it may not be authentic (James 3:17).

- Has this dream or spiritual manifestation caused you and others to want to glorify God more? Is Jesus the center of your experience, or are you the center? It is very clear from the Bible that Jesus expected manifestations given in the spiritual realm to keep Him always as the center. All biblically sound, spiritual experiences are Christ-centered (1 Cor. 12:1-3; John 14-16).

- Did this experience cause you to be respectful of others, or did it cause you to feel superior? If it caused you to feel spiritually above others, it may not have been a legitimate manifestation. The dream itself may call you to be tempered and tried until you have humility to match the gift.

- Are you willing to submit your experience to the scrutiny of your pastor and other peers? If not, your experience should be suspect (1 Cor. 14).

- Has this manifestation or insight strengthened your commitment to Christ, His church and the foundational truths of Christianity? No legitimate experience or gift will take you to extremes or violate basic doctrine. If you are called to start your own little club with those who agree with you, you ought to suspect your dream or vision. It probably isn't authentic (Deut. 18:9-22).

- Has this experience caused you to be more concerned about others? If so, this experience is producing the kind of fruit that is biblical and legitimate (1 Cor. 12-14).

- Has this spiritual event caused you to walk in harmony with Christ? If feelings of superiority occur as a result of your experience, it may not be valid (1 Cor. 12).

- Is this experience open to anyone? If you feel it is only for you, it's probably not legitimate or genuine. God is no respecter of persons when it comes to spiritual experiences (Acts 10:34-36).

I use this checklist regularly to evaluate inspirations, visions and dreams that I and others around me have.

HOW IMPORTANT WERE DREAMS IN THE BIBLE?

The Bible describes dreams from three origins: 1) natural (Eccl. 5:3), 2) divine (Gen. 28:12) and 3) evil (Deut. 13:1-2; Jer. 23:32).

Dreaming, in the biblical sense, allows the human

mind to enter into the realm of the infinite. The Bible says that the era we live in (the era of Pentecost) is the era of the dreamers. "Your young men will see visions, your old men will dream dreams" (Acts 2:17).

Dreams played a big role in the incarnation as well. The following warnings, instructions and appearances of angels all occurred in dreams.

- An angel told Joseph about Mary's conception of the Christ (Matt. 1:20-23).

- The wise men were warned not to return to Herod (Matt. 2:12).

- Joseph was instructed to flee to Egypt with Mary and Jesus (Matt. 2:13).

- An angel told Joseph to return to Israel from Egypt (Matt. 2:19-20).

- Joseph was warned that Archelaus reined over Judea in place of his father, Herod, so Joseph took his family to Galilee (Matt. 2:22).

- The wife of Pilate suffered in a dream over Jesus' sentence (Matt. 27:19).

We dare not scoff at dreaming, but we also need to commit ourselves to true biblical evaluation. I learned a few things about handling dreams from Joseph and from personal experience.

1. Don't share them too quickly.

If there's any mistake dreamers make when God tells them something, it is that they share it too quickly. The only solace I have is that God used Joseph — even though he had the same flaw. But it seems like those of us who share things too quickly often experience a great deal more pain in the supernatural.

I've learned I'll probably make mistakes, but God can use mistakes to fulfill the dream. To me, Christians seem to be getting more and more uptight over the years. With a bit more perfectionism in our ranks, we ought to be able to stymie any work of the Holy Spirit.

2. All dreams need the tension of rejection.

Criticism helps us grow far more than praise does. As you gradually share your dream, you will find plenty of critics, as Joseph did. They may be annoying or discouraging, but you need them. They refine our dreams. They test them. They weed out our pride and character flaws and eventually leave us with the authentic dream.

3. It's best to concentrate on dreams that apply to you.

A friend of mine humorously described a "special" gift God gave him as a new believer — the ability to recognize faults in others within thirty seconds of meeting them. People are too often ready to accept supernatural messages that correct anybody but them.

A year ago I was invited to a prayer meeting that was held on a yacht. I was a little nervous about it because of the starry-eyed look in the eyes of a couple of the fellows. After two days of praying and seeking the Lord, one of them told me, "I have a vision about you. There are worms crawling throughout your body and out of your head. The Lord says that if you'll confess what the source of them is, you'll be freed."

Now I don't mind confessing my faults. I had two problems with the message, though.

The idea of having worms crawling out of my head didn't make me feel real safe. Second, I really couldn't think of anything that matched his descriptions. So I told him, "I'm sorry, but I think you're wrong."

I explained, "First, what you're sharing doesn't come in the tone and spirit that I have learned to recognize as the Holy Spirit. He doesn't have to guess at what's wrong. He knows. And He usually doesn't emphasize what's wrong. He usually comes with an appeal or invitation to move toward what's right.

"A second problem I have is that I don't know you. You don't know my life, and I don't know your life. It is essential to know the track record and character of the messenger before accepting the message.

"Third, I think the Lord would probably have you concentrate on any faults you have before He would have you concentrate on my faults. I remember reading somewhere about making sure you get the telephone pole out of your eye before you worry about the speck of sawdust in your brother's eye."

I've determined that when it comes to my dreaming, the best response is to concentrate on what applies to me. Although God could speak to other people through my dreams, I believe it is the exception, not the rule. The best way I can help someone else is by serving them or by being a good example for them.

A Few Things Dreams Are Not

In this chapter on supernatural dreams, I've discussed the physical and spiritual aspects of dreaming. Dreams are often like seeds, which we need to cover with soil and cultivate before they come to fruition. If we think we have received a supernatural dream, we need to test its validity, and I have suggested some guidelines to do that. To help us understand dreams further, I also described the importance of dreams in the Bible and what we can learn from Joseph's dreams. To close this chapter, I will further refine our definition of supernatural dreams by listing some things that dreams are *not*.

- A biblical dream is not an amazing pathway to riches.

  We Americans are prone to power, riches and fame dreaming. I'll admit, like you, that I would rather have abundance than poverty. I would rather be ahead than behind. However, that isn't necessarily the way God always leads. A real biblical dream might call you to poverty. I'm inspired by dreamers such as Mother Teresa who were called to give everything to serve the poor.

  On the other hand, some characters have gone overboard on poverty. One guy lived on a platform on top of a pole for thirty years. He said God told him to do it. I question that kind of dream. It doesn't seem to benefit others or glorify God.

- Receiving a biblical dream does not make you superior.

  I believe that Christians are called to collaborative team ministry. A biblical dream simply gives you assurance of your place in God's plan. The team spirit of the body of Christ is demonstrated in Acts 13:2, where the Holy Spirit said, "Set apart for me Barnabas and Saul for the work to which I have called them." The other prophets and teachers who were at the prayer meeting joined together to send the new missionary team forth with prayer and fasting.

- A biblical dream isn't something you can choose to have.

  I've read material and attended several seminars that purport to teach a person how to prophesy or dream. That stuff scares me. I think our assignment is to be open. Joseph only had two God-given dreams in his 110 years (that we know of), so I think we in the twentieth-century church should not feel anxious about whether or not God speaks to us in dreams.

- God is not a gossip.

  He respects you far too much to spread around your dirty laundry. If God can communicate with you directly, He will not use other people's dreams to expose your sins.

- We all receive our dreams and supernatural experiences differently.

  I've asked a number of people who have the gift of prophecy how they receive their prophecies. I've noted they all receive their gift in vastly different ways. I've asked preachers how they get their sermons. One guy I know says he gets them on the golf course. I believe it.

  I've learned I receive my sermons by preparing months ahead. I don't actually study for specific themes anymore. I just study. I read three or four books a week dealing with a variety of topics. I find that when the Holy Spirit gives me a clear theme, then I can use the notes I've collected. At the same time, a prophecy will often come.

Though a person who is deaf from birth can only dream with sight and touch, the experience is still a dream. This illustrates God's ability to work in the arena of our understanding and experience. Regardless of your past experience, God can use a dream to speak to you if your heart is open.

* God speaks more in general notions than in great detail.

I wouldn't say either of Joseph's dreams was vividly detailed. There was a lot of guesswork left in those dreams. After all, how would you interpret your brothers' sheaves bowing to your sheaf? And what would be the meaning of the sun, moon and stars bowing down? I think dreams in the supernatural are intended to alert our ears, eyes and hearts so we will watch more closely for the will of God.

God doesn't hand us road maps; He points in directions. When He spoke to Abraham, He didn't say, "Take Highway 61, then turn on Highway 21." He simply pointed in a direction and said, "Go, leave the clan behind and listen closely." A dream points you in the right direction.

But what happens if the people around you say you're headed in the wrong direction?

In the next chapter we'll see why religious people can be so mean.

FIVE

WHY ARE RELIGIOUS PEOPLE SO MEAN?

When his brothers saw that their father loved him more than any of them, they hated him and could not speak a kind word to him (Gen. 37:4).

Here comes that dreamer...Come now, let's kill him and throw him into one of these cisterns (Gen. 37:19).

SCENE: *Reuben's tent, some years before 1687 B.C.*

REUBEN: I was once a dreamer. I am the oldest, the firstborn to Leah. The whole family knows that my grandfather Laban tricked my father into marrying my mother. My father seemed to resent this all of his life. But he was kind to me because I was the oldest. He gave me a strong name — Reuben.

But I was so angry at my father. I slept with his concubine, Bilhah. It was a way to get even, I thought. In reality it marked the end of my dreams. But I never meant to harm Joseph, his favorite son.

I was such a coward! I should have been able to stop my brothers from selling him — even if he was an arrogant so-and-so. But they all mocked me behind my back. They knew I had betrayed our father before.

Why did jealousy burn so hot within us? I suppose it was because we all had our dreams, but we had lost them. There was a look in Joseph's eyes that told us he would never let go of his.

There I stood in my father's tent, holding a piece of Joseph's coat with goat's blood spattered on it. I didn't really lie. Our father just assumed that Joseph had been killed by a wild animal. And I, the oldest son, didn't even have the courage to tell him the truth — that Joseph was still alive.

SCENE: *Church in California (conservative persuasion), pastor's study.*

PASTOR: Hello, Jim? I need help. *(To himself)* I've got to hold these tears back. I wonder if he can sense the tightness in my voice? I feel like I have a giant chicken bone stuck sideways in my throat. Tommy, my only son. How could he do such a thing?

Yes, I need some help, Jim. Yes, it's serious. No, I haven't fallen. No, all has been going well in the church. Yes, I'll tell Jill hi.

Jim, I've lost the church. No, my speaking has been better than ever. It's Tommy. He was arrested by the police with a number of his friends for smoking marijuana in the parking lot of the church.

The board fired me last night. They said I was an embarrassment as a pastor.

We've worked so hard with Tommy. These older guys just don't understand what it's like raising a kid today. Besides that, Tommy is twenty-two. I don't know what they expect me to do.

Our new building plans were coming along so well. We've raised three quarters of the money already. We're winning more and more people to Christ.

I've decided to just pack my bags and leave, Jim. I've put away a few dollars. We should be OK. I think I'll just go to the mountains, live in a cabin, read my Bible and love Christ.

A *Seattle Times* columnist named Jennifer James recently wrote an article titled "A Mean Spirit Seems to Be Hampering Society's Growth."[1] Her insights are always powerful and accurate. In the article she stated: "What motivates an individual motivates a culture." If individuals are mean, society will be mean.

It is my observation that the church is becoming more and more a mean society. In her book *Sold Into Egypt*, Madeleine L'Engle quotes the first lines of Tolstoy's *Anna Karenina*: "Happy families are all alike. And every unhappy family is unhappy in its own way."[2] I've found that far too many churches are unhappy in their own ways.

We Americans can tell when we need a kinder, gentler

nation and society. We need a kinder, gentler church, too.

Read Genesis 37 and compare yourself to Joseph's brothers. See how they react to his dream — with jealousy, violence and lies. Do you see yourself in them?

The church is becoming progressively more effective at driving out most of its dreamers. I think it is an overreaction to the self-destructing saints on TV who have tainted our message. A low self-esteem in the church is causing us to massacre anyone who would dare dream.

The church ought to be the friendliest place on earth to dreamers and their dreams, especially to those who have failed. Our hearts are called to make room for those who might be considered "irregular" people.

The gift of encouragement is a highly valued gift in the Bible. Dreamers need encouragement more than rebuke most of the time. Here are some specific times in my life when I needed to be encouraged.

- I am living through those I-don't-want-to times. Sometimes I don't want to follow God's dreams, and I certainly don't want to obey Him. I have friends who gently exhort me in those times. I hope you do, too.

- At other times I experience a Romans 7 dilemma. This is an I-want-to time. However, when I am really ready to go for it — and go for it hard — I discover that I don't have the strength to do what I want to do. At those times I need encouragement from others and a touch from God.

- There are also I-can't times. You've had those times, and so have I. It's a situation where we simply can't do God's will, because of either poor character or addictive patterns in our own lives. This is the reason we really need recovery groups inside the church.

A dreamer sometimes experiences the most pain from the Reuben types in the church. They are the one-time dreamers who disappear when others are tearing us apart.

Not long ago I was in a group that was discussing the escapades of a Christian leader whose fall had been recorded in the press. None of us knew the person, but we were going on and on about his purported life-style.

Finally, one of the men said, "This conversation is wrong, and I don't want to be a part of it."

We all stopped. I was embarrassed that I hadn't spoken up earlier. On the other hand, a Reuben would have said, "Hey, don't kill him, but if you want to maim him and throw him in a pit, that's fine. He's not my friend." We all repented and moved on to other more positive topics.

HOW DID WE GET SO MEAN?

Why is the church so mean? is a great question. But let's personalize it and ask, Why are you and I so mean?

Much of our mean-spiritedness comes from comparing ourselves with others. It's tough when the standards of obedience come from comparison. When comparison enters the ranks of the church rather than team collaboration, dreamers must be driven out.

A second cause of meanness is that we have a poverty mentality. Stephen Covey in his recent book *Principle Centered Leadership* says, "There are three ways you can spot greatness. It comes from a *commitment to integrity* (meaning being who you are and being the same in private or in public); a *commitment to maturity*, which means being fully who you are; an *abundance mentality*."[3]

Joseph's brothers definitely had a poverty mentality as opposed to an abundance mentality. They didn't believe there was enough inheritance to go around after Joseph got his cut. I see plenty of this in the church too.

I recently received a letter from a person in our church who had left the music department. She had concluded that only those who had released records were able to sing in our church.

The root of the complaint was a real and painful fear that there might not be enough opportunity to go around. That poverty mentality had stolen this person's dream of involvement in the music department.

I believe a third cause for meanness is the fear of not being loved. Joseph's brothers had not been properly loved by their father, Jacob, due to his preference for Rachel and his resentment of Leah. If Joseph's brothers had been confident that their father loved them, they would not have feared his apparent favorite.

Do you understand that your Father God loves you fully? I understand that in part. I now recognize that when I give in to fears that lead to meanness, I have forgotten who my Father is and that He has more than enough of everything to go around.

None of Joseph's brothers had dreams of their own, because they hated Joseph's dreams. Keeping your dreams will mean enjoying the dreams of others.

A fourth recent source of meanness in the church has come as a reaction to the fall of Christian leaders in our country. If the apostle Paul were alive today, however, I don't think he'd be surprised by the scandals. You see, he lived in a "Corinthianized" culture as well. A Corinthianized culture is one driven by lust and materialism, as was the biblical city of old. A Corinthianized culture will produce its share of Corinthian-type sins in its leaders.

As a result, lay leaders are rising up with the intent of protecting the church from its pastors. While their motives are good, their fears often cause them to be suspicious and mean-spirited. While there is a time for speaking "tough truth," there is also a time for encouragement, love, acceptance and forgiveness.

One thing I appreciated about my mentor and great

friend Jamie Buckingham is that he never really wrote off anybody when they failed. He was always able to separate the person's sins from the person. It's a lesson I've tried to practice.

ARE YOU MEAN-SPIRITED?

Here's a brief meanness quiz. Take it quick and bear it.

- Do you find yourself giving twice as many criticisms as compliments? If so, you might be a dream-stealer.

- Has anyone left your circle of fellowship without talking with you? Give them a call and ask them why they left. You may learn a lot about yourself and your church. (Lately I've been encouraging churches to give exit interviews.)

- Have you decided that the church is a bunch of hypocrites and that the place for you is in the safety of your own prayer closet at home? If so, you might simply be hurt. Perhaps you have had your own dreams destroyed. Be careful that you don't do the same thing to others.

- Have you ever dropped your teacher or pastor a note that just said, "Hey, good job!"? If not, you may be silently contributing to the demise of some great dream.

- What is your first reaction to a new vision or dream at your church? Is it: Wouldn't it be exciting to see that occur! Or do you think of all the details that it would take to fulfill it? Or, worse yet, do you privately start adding up how much it will cost you?

- Have you forgotten that the gifted people you know have feelings? Sometimes we forget that some of the people we honor in the body of Christ are actually people. We throw them into the pit too quickly. OK, some of them may be annoying, but no one deserves the pit.

No one could pass this little quiz with a perfect score, including me. At the same time, I know that I myself have been a victim of meanness, as I'm sure you have been too. The good news is that we can take steps to make a change in the church.

TURNING THE TREND

If your dreams have been criticized and you would like to turn around the spirit of meanness in the church, begin with yourself. Here are some strategies that will help.

- Respond in the opposite spirit. When criticized, respond with appreciation. When on the receiving end of anger, respond with peace. When taken for granted, respond with thanks.

- Recognize any fears in your own heart and replace them with an understanding of God's love. Remind yourself that He has plenty of dreams to go around.

- If you are in the pit, thank Him for it. Sure, there may even be a few Reubens standing around, letting your brothers massacre you. But know that good will come from it.

- Thank God for all the pain-givers. They mean it for evil, but, as we see in Joseph's life, God means it for good.

- Remind yourself that a dream from God is bigger than anyone's attempt to kill it.

- Remember that the source of the mean-spiritedness around you may be found in your own heart. Be humble. Be willing to change. Become committed to creating a dreamer-friendly environment.

- Remember that a dreamer-friendly environment is comfortable with failure. It embraces the one who failed and expects successes to grow from the ashes of defeat. Verbalize your expectation that ashes will be turned to beauty and ruins into an architectural masterpiece.

REVIEW

Before moving on, let us reconsider the four reasons why dreamers become dream-killers.

1. An identity built on comparison to others.

2. A poverty mentality (the fear that there is not enough).

3. The fear of not being loved.

4. A reaction to past failures.

SIX

DOES GOD
HAVE FAVORITES?

Now Israel loved Joseph more than any of his
other sons, because he had been born to him in
his old age; and he made a richly ornamented
robe for him (Gen. 37:3).

SCENE: *Israel's tent, 1703 B.C.*

JACOB: Wild animals! Wild animals have stolen my
son from me. My God has taken him! Elo-
him, why do You always take or withhold the
thing that means the most to me?
     Joseph — such an astounding child! I re-
member the day I gave him his robe. The

gold and silver trim neatly fit to his ankles and wrists. The coat was a sign that he would be my inheritor. I assumed all my sons would accept that Joseph would be my favorite because he was Rachel's son.

My brother, Esau, reminded me about what the quest for favoritism had done in our childhood home. It turned us against one another in hate. It turned my mother and me into deceivers. But I couldn't help it. Joseph was my favorite. But did I have to make it so obvious?

I can't help but see how delighted my sons are that Joseph is gone. Except for Reuben. But, then again, he may just feel guilty about Bilhah.

I loved them all as well as I could, but Joseph was my favorite. He will never be replaced!

FATHERS AND SONS

"Pastor, I can't trust God."

"Why not?" I asked.

"I don't know why. In fact, I'm annoyed whenever we read the Lord's prayer or I hear others talking about their families."

"Do you always feel a little different from other people?" I asked, suspecting that I was dealing with the syndrome of the adult children of alcoholics (ACOA).

"Yes," he said.

"May I ask a very personal question, Jim? Was your father an alcoholic?"

"Yes, he was."

"Tell me a little about your life."

Jim proceeded to tell me of multiple occasions when his father had promised gifts and trips and failed to deliver.

"Are you afraid that God won't keep His promises, too, Jim?"

"I don't know." He began to get choked up.

I told him that it was entirely possible that his experiences with his natural father had affected his image of his heavenly Father. I had seen many cases before where the dysfunctionality of the home impacted people spiritually.

"Jim, I would encourage you to get into our support groups on Tuesday night. You will find other adults who have some of these same traits: always feeling different, unable to trust leaders, unable to anticipate the joy of goals completed because you are certain nothing will work out anyway.

"You need a new father, Jim. I found in the story of Gideon that the Holy Spirit's first assignment for him was to tear down his father's idols. I take this to mean the Holy Spirit's assignment is to lead us to correct all those false images of God that are imposed on us by our fathers."

"That makes sense," Jim responded.

"It will be a hard struggle, but I've seen success over and over again. A dysfunction in your family can affect your ability to believe in God. It affects your ability to dream."

In our closing prayer he even confessed that he felt that God loved his friends more than He loved him. As Jim left the office, I prayed that God would heal the pain he felt.

IS IT POSSIBLE TO ESCAPE YOUR FAMILY OF ORIGIN?

After months of meditating on the life of Joseph, I've wondered whether God sent him to Egypt partially to get him away from his relatives.

If you want to talk about the quintessential dysfunctional family, Joseph's had to be it. Multiple mothers and concubines filled the household with suffocating tension. There was tension between the oldest son, Reuben, and the favorite son, Joseph. Jacob was obviously unequal in his dispersion of affection. And, for certain, Jacob's tricky nature would have had the sons explaining for him over and over again, not unlike a child in our society explaining the behavior of his alcoholic father.

Almost all of us are products of dysfunctional families. Someone has joked that 98 percent of us come from dysfunctional homes, and the other 2 percent are in denial. Without a doubt, our personalities are shaped by genetics and environment. Your family of origin may also affect your ability to dream and the way in which you carry out your dreams.

You see, we all carry our homes in our hearts. It really wasn't that God needed to get Joseph away from his family; God needed Joseph to come to terms with the family in his heart.

There are steps you can take to live and dream deliberately free from the family dysfunction in your past. I've seen numbers of people during the past few years come to grips with patterns such as ACOA or absentee fathers and the pain that they caused in childhood. It seems that those of us born in the postwar era often experienced an absence of both father and mother, which gave us great pain. It is one of the reasons why the American Medical Association is recommending that mothers, if at all possible, stay home until their children are at least five years old.

Here are some practical steps I have found for recovering from a dysfunctional family and making yourself available for God's dreams.

- Forgive your father and mother.

- If you are dealing with alcoholism, join a support group that deals with real issues of ACOA.

- Become part of a small group. Share your feelings openly in an environment that is filled with acceptance and forgiveness.

- Choose to live deliberately rather than emotionally.

- Watch for signs that you may be affecting your own children's dreams and abilities to dream in the same way your parents affected you.

- Accept the fact that everyone has suffered from an imperfect parenting experience and run to Father God with the power of the Holy Spirit as your new reference point. Study the Bible with His generous Fatherhood in mind.

I've found these steps are necessary to remove some of the distortions to sound thinking. I have no doubt that the dysfunctional environment in which Joseph found himself crippled the power of his dream. As the brothers fought for attention from a father who obviously had distanced himself, nothing but pain could arise. And in a family filled with one-upmanship, the spirit of servanthood was unknown.

THE SPIRIT OF SERVANTHOOD IN A DREAM

I have come to see that a common trait of children from a dysfunctional home is the quest to be the favorite, the most powerful, the best, the richest. No Christian dream will work with these goals. It is only in the spirit of servanthood that dreams are fulfilled.

Joseph would learn that God has no favorites. Jacob may have had favorites, but God has no favorites. He only has participants in His great dream, and there's enough of His dream to go around. By the end of his life, Joseph understood this. As the tribes moved into Goshen, he could see they all had a place to live, they all had wealth, and they all prospered. All of us have only part of the dream.

Selfish dreaming comes from a micro-vision that fits our smallness of heart. God's kind of dreaming rises from a macro-vision of what He is up to.

An observer walked up to a bricklayer and asked him what he was doing.

"I'm building a wall," he responded.

Walking on to the bricklayer's assistant, who was mixing cement with all of his might, the observer asked, "And what are you doing?"

"I'm building a cathedral," he responded.

We have a choice to rejoice with God's macro-vision or to grumble with our micro-vision.

I had occasion when Billy Graham held his crusade in Seattle two years ago to serve as one of the leaders of the team. I was impressed over and over again by the servant attitude of those who served around him. I had no doubt that they exemplified the true spirit of Billy Graham.

How stunned I was as a pastor when, several weeks before the crusade, Graham sent questionnaires to pastors in our city, asking us what we felt he should preach about when he came. I'll never forget his words: "I am called by God to serve what He is doing through you in your city."

We have been called to dream through serving, not through being served. We've been called through powerlessness, not powerfulness. It is no wonder that Billy Graham has stayed free from scandal and is referred to as the "prophet with honor."

I want to be that kind of dreamer.

THE MANGER MESSAGE

Christ's servant attitude was apparent from His first breath drawn in the stable in Bethlehem.

The angels gathered, the plan was set.
All of heaven gathered to see the babe at His
    marvelous birth.
All had their assignments; all were on alert.
The great white steed was pastured and never
    to be heard,
And the scepter had been stored and put away
    for another time.

This was a slave's birth — the battle cry of
    heaven, a child's helpless whimper.
These were heaven's weapons of choice.
Cheers arose at His first cry.
Some angels even broke forth in praise so
    strong it spilled over onto a field with
    shepherds at work.
Armorless, yet fearless, the Savior was born,
Not a single flex of strength but only the vul-
    nerable stretch of a baby's arm,
No attending army, only the presence of a
    mother's deep love,
Not equipped but emptied, not ruling but serv-
    ing,
This child was born.

The crown left with robe folded, the manger
    with hay adorned,
The Savior, the only Savior, as a baby was born.
The logic of heaven, born — to lose is to gain, to
    serve is to rule, to give is to receive.
And to die is to live.

No books ever to be written or songs that he
    would sing,
A message, a simple message, the kind only a
    manger could send.

A message loud with pounding volumes of this
    divine love. A message still ringing, a
    message still heard.
Come home, come home no matter what you've
    done.
Come home...
I heard it in His whimper.
I saw it in His blood.
I feel it in His presence and know it as His love.

— Doug Murren

Paul described Christ's *kenosis*, or emptiness, and laid down a solid pattern for servanthood. Here's what a God-inspired dreamer looks like.

Make my joy complete by being like-minded, having the same love, being one in spirit and purpose. Do nothing out of selfish ambition or vain conceit, but in humility consider others better than yourselves. Each of you should look not only to your own interests, but also to the interests of others.

Your attitude should be the same as that of Christ Jesus:

Who, being in very nature God,
did not consider equality with God something
    to be grasped,
but made himself nothing, taking the very na-
    ture of a servant,
being made in human likeness.
And being found in appearance as a man,
he humbled himself
and became obedient to death —
even death on a cross!

Therefore, God exalted him to the highest place
and gave him the name that is above every
     name,
that at the name of Jesus every knee should
     bow,
in heaven and on earth and under the earth,
and every tongue confess that Jesus Christ is
     Lord,
to the glory of God the Father (Phil. 2:2-11).

SELF-SERVING DREAMS

A middle-aged woman stumbled onto our grounds not many months ago. Dazed, emotionally and mentally drained and apparently suicidal, she stepped into our counseling office and pleaded for help.

A pastor began to interview her about her health and about events in her life. But she kept crying, "God has let me down. God has let me down."

She had been in despair over her husband when she flipped on the television to watch "Success-N-Life" with Robert Tilton. Supposedly a word of the Lord came over the air. Someone was being called to give a thousand dollars to Tilton's dream. If that person gave the money, her husband would stay with her.

The woman sent the money. Nevertheless, her husband ran off with another woman and filed for divorce within days of her sending the thousand dollars. She was a thousand dollars poorer and had lost hope in God because of someone who used others to serve his dream. A God-given dream will serve others — not the dreamer.

CONCLUSION

When portions were served to them [Joseph's brothers] from Joseph's table, Benjamin's portion was five times as much as anyone else's. So they feasted and drank freely with him (Gen. 43:34).

At this time Joseph is second in Egypt only to the pharaoh. His brothers have come to him to buy food, but they do not recognize him after so many years of separation. Joseph has one final test for them. It hinges on the dysfunction that he knows has crippled their dreams in the past.

When Joseph recognized his brothers on their first visit to Egypt, he questioned them thoroughly concerning the rest of the family. He learned that his father and Benjamin, his full brother, were still alive.

On his brothers' second visit, they were required to bring their younger brother, Benjamin. Benjamin became a test of their character.

Joseph invited his brothers to dine with him. Though he seated them in order of their age, Benjamin's portion was five times larger than his brothers' portions. Joseph had no desire to show favoritism. Rather he wanted to see whether his brothers had been broken of the dysfunction of favoritism. He had discovered servanthood. Had they?

The Scriptures do not record any reaction among Joseph's brothers to Benjamin's extra portion. However, Judah passionately pleaded on Benjamin's behalf when Joseph threatened to retain him in Egypt. It seems that the quarreling brothers had finally learned some consideration for their father's feelings. They had learned to serve the family instead of themselves.

LIFE APPLICATION

Do you cringe when you see others' dreams advancing instead of your own? Does it bother you when other people receive recognition when you know you deserve it as well?

I think most of us would say yes to those questions, at least for some situations. These are the kinds of questions that keep us in tune as dreamers. We need to be the kind of people who invite God to give our brothers and sisters a portion that is five times greater than our own. This is a quality of a great dreamer and the sign of a great heart.

SEVEN

WHY AREN'T
DREAMS EASY?

He called down famine on the land and destroyed all their supplies of food; and he sent a
man before them — Joseph, sold as a slave. They
bruised his feet with shackles, his neck was put
in irons, till what he foretold came to pass, till
the word of the Lord proved him true (Ps.
105:16-19).

I once heard Jamie Buckingham talk about dreaming,
which he loved to do, with a group of pastors. It reminded
me of a section in his book *Where Eagles Soar*.

My friend Peter Lord, pastor of the Park Avenue

Baptist Church in Titusville, Florida, is one of the few men I know who has designed his life so his first priority is to abide with God. As a result, he is constantly probing those of us around him to realign our priorities. Last year Peter and I joined our old friend Mickey Evans on a three-day hunting and camping trip together in the Everglades. Each of us brought a son to share in the time of fellowship. One afternoon Peter and I sat under an oak tree while our sons wandered off into a deep hammock [grove] looking for wild turkey. Peter, who came to the United States from Jamaica, began his usual spiritual probing.

"Don't give me your answers," Peter said. "Just think about them as I ask you five questions."

Peter's first question was this: *Why did God make you?* I knew what he was driving at. He wanted me to define why I was here. What was the reason for my creation? What was my primary reason for being on earth? If the primary purpose of a pen is to write, if the primary purpose of a chair is to provide seating, if the primary purpose of a trombone is to make music — then what was my primary purpose for being on earth? I made a mental note — true to the Westminster Confession: I am here to glorify God and enjoy Him forever.

Second: *What is the thing you love more than anything else?* I was tempted to give a religious answer, but I knew better. One of the best ways to test your greatest love is to determine what you can't do without. I have a friend whose greatest love is his head of hair. He won't even let his elders put their hands on his head for fear they'll mess up his hair. I did not think I was that vain. Inwardly I answered: My greatest love is my family.

Peter's third question: *What is your greatest fear?* Again, I was tempted to give a religious answer about being delivered from fear — but that's just not so. In fact, everyone is afraid of something. My greatest fear, I thought, was losing my family and being left without their love.

Fourth: *What is your greatest ambition?* Deeply spiritual people are always ambitious people. Not worldly or egotistical ambition but an ambition sanctified and restored to its proper dimension. Peter was asking about my goal in life. That was easy. For years, ever since I started writing professionally, I yearned to write a book that would touch the world for Jesus Christ.

Finally, Peter asked: *Why do you want God?* That took more thinking than the rest. He was asking, in essence, what I expected to gain by being a Christian. That was easy: I wanted God so He could help me accomplish my goal for Him — for without Him I was nothing.

All my answers seemed sound. At least I seemed to have my spiritual pyramid down pat: God first, family next, career last.

"If your answer to question number one is not the same as your answer to question number four, you are a mixed-up person," Peter said matter-of-factly.

He continued. "If God made you to harvest apples, and you are busy planting oranges, you are going to be confused when it comes time to pick the fruit."

"But I said my reason for being on earth is to glorify God and enjoy Him forever."

"That's fine," Peter answered. "Then your greatest ambition had better be to glorify God and enjoy Him forever."

But I had not said that. I had said my ambition was to do something for Him, rather than to abide in Him — to have fellowship with Him. Slowly it dawned on me. I am here on this earth for no other reason but to have communion with Him and to renew that wonderful relationship that took place in the Garden of Eden when Adam walked alone with God in the cool of the evening.

If I have any ambition other than that, I am missing God's purpose for my life. If I have been placed on this earth to abide in God, then my greatest ambition should be to have fellowship with Him.

Peter continued: "Your answer to question number two ought to be the same as your answer to question number three."

Again I was trapped. I had the right sequence, but the wrong answers.[1]

The reason Peter Lord's questions are so pertinent to dreaming is because they caused Jamie to stumble across a truth: None of us is really an adequate dreamer. That's why we need testing. It isn't the dream that gets tested — it's the dreamer. When God gives a dream, there's nothing wrong with it. But the dreamer probably needs a lot of work. I'm convinced that dreams come to test and shape our character.

Whenever you and I get a true dream from God, that dream, by the power of the Holy Spirit, immediately begins to shape us to fit it. Some therefore would say that our dreams should match our character types and our personal spiritual giftings. I think there's a great deal of wisdom there. The likelihood of failure increases the further we move away from our talents.

However, I think matching the call to the personality can be overdone. Often I think the office makes the person — for example, when someone is elected president of the United States. Furthermore, I'm not going to pretend to restrict God in the kinds of dreams He gives.

YOUR DREAM WILL TEST YOU

One reliable sign that a dream is from God is that it doesn't work out easily. The dream itself may even anger you because you're taking all the tests but not seeing any fulfillment of the dream. Take heart — Joseph was tested in prison for years before there was any positive movement toward his dream.

I know a pastor named Wayne Gordon who lives in Chicago. He's the only white pastor for miles and miles in the ghetto section of East Chicago.

Wayne first went into the ghettos of Chicago as a student at Wheaton College. Then he became a football coach and eventually opened an outreach gymnasium, a clinic and a church. He also buys condemned buildings, restores them and turns them into condominiums to be sold at reasonable prices to the homeless.

I once asked Wayne whether he felt safe. He said he really did.

"Have you ever been robbed?" I asked.

"Twelve times," he said. The first time was on his wedding night. "They broke into our house and stole all of our money. I asked my wife then if she still wanted to be my wife. She said she was certain she loved me and she wanted to be part of my dream." Then he laughed and said, "I haven't asked her the same question the last eleven times."

WHY THE TESTING?

There are at least two reasons why we need to be tested.

1. We need to be tested so our character will match our dreams. When he was seventeen years old, Joseph's character certainly didn't match his dreams. But after a few years as a slave and a few more years as a prisoner, he had some character to work with. God is as interested in who you become while you are dreaming as He is that your dream becomes a reality.

2. Tests remind us that God's dreams are bigger than we are. Good dreams lead you to this conviction: I need God.

My friend and fellow preaching-team member Mike Meeks recently shared a powerful message. He said that God has a test for every one of us that we are not equal to. I was taken aback because I had always believed on the basis of 1 Corinthians 10:13 that God would never let us be tempted beyond what we are able to handle. Sensing our objection to the sermon, Mike went on: "I'm not talking about temptation. I'm talking about a testing that will show you that you are weak, but His grace is sufficient [see 2 Cor. 11:30]. We all need a test bigger than we are to show us our need of God so we can experience the peaceful wonder of what it is to rely on Him."

LIFE APPLICATION

Dreams are tricky. Sometimes you're in the middle of a test and you don't even know it. Here are some subtle things that can test your dream and some ways to deal with them.

- Other people seem jealous of what God is doing in your life.

   It's easier to deal with these attacks if you realize they are probably the result of misunderstandings. For example, I have been accused of being prideful when in actuality my aloofness came from being introverted.

- You have the feeling that God has special people and that you are one of them.

    When you feel this attitude cropping up inside you, you can be sure it does not come from God. You need to revise your perspective on what makes a person special.

A few years ago a friend of mine asked me to visit his son in prison. My friend was a man of honor, a hard-working and honest man. I sensed his pain about having a son incarcerated.

I was shocked when I met the young man. His teeth were partially rotten from drug use. His attention span had been greatly hampered. He looked like any derelict you would see on the street. There was one difference. I knew how much this young man's father loved him.

Since then I've been careful about judging derelicts quickly. I have reminded myself that somewhere they have a mother, father or grandparent who cares about them.

That incident has convinced me that all people are special, but no one is any more special than others.

KEYS TO PASSING THE TESTS

Here are some keys I have found that will help you face testings and temptations as you continue in your dream.

- Make sure you measure progress. This has helped me a number of times to answer the enemy when the test of patience has gotten to me.

- Practice the habit of daily discipline. Five

chapters of the Bible a day with fifteen to twenty minutes of prayer will quickly develop into a valuable habit.

- Rejoice in others' blessings. It helps you to enjoy your own even more.

- Have a group of people to whom you can confess your failures and shortcomings. This will keep guilt from taking you off track.

- Anytime you get a dream or vision, sit down and count the cost first. This way mounting costs won't surprise you or keep you from seeing a dream fulfilled.

- Know that God Himself is never really testing or trying you. It is your own need for character development that is indeed trying you.

The year 1991 was a time of extreme testing for me. There was a great deal of illness in our family. With the national recession, finances in our church were also challenged.

By the end of that year my family received a diagnosis of the problem, and healing occurred. Our church also finished with a 20 percent increase in income over the previous year. But the testings and challenges throughout the year were great.

A close friend of mine who knew the level of pressure I had been under said, "I can't believe how well you stood up under the pressure."

At first I thought, Maybe I'm just a strong person.

I meditated on the comment later and concluded that God helped me stand under excruciating pressure from all sides because I had built the daily disciplines I shared with you. Now I know my future holds even greater testings and trials for some of the dreams I'm seeing. I know that the size of the test matches the dimensions of the dream (and I'm dreaming some pretty big dreams). I shudder to think that I should fail. Nonetheless, I'm committed to those simple disciplines every day. I'm counting on the testings but trusting Christ.

If your dream is

- to have a great marriage,
- to build a great church,
- to raise great kids or
- to build a great Christian business founded on Christian principles,

you will be tested. Don't be surprised by testings, but be transformed by them.

EIGHT

THE VALUE OF A PIT

So when the Midianite merchants came by, his brothers pulled Joseph up out of the cistern and sold him for twenty shekels of silver to the Ishmaelites, who took him to Egypt (Gen. 37:28).

Then they got Joseph's robe, slaughtered a goat and dipped the robe in the blood (Gen. 37:31).

SCENE: *Pharaoh's palace, sometime around 1690 B.C.*

JOSEPH: I still dream of that coat. They don't even know my real name here, nor would they care about the story of a robe that meant so much in the life of a seventeen-year-old boy in Canaan who's not alive anymore.

The Egyptians call me Zaphenath-Paneah. I'm thirty years old now — and finally free. What I wouldn't give to see that robe again. It was a symbol of my inheritance, but to me it was a symbol of dominance. Father meant well, but there was a lot of harm done with that garment of honor.

Since then I've learned how to serve. I've served Potiphar, I've served the prison warden and I've served Pharaoh. But most of all I serve my God.

I guess no man can serve God in an ornamented coat.

Every dreamer knows how the inside of a pit is decorated. It's dark and has slimy sides — in Joseph's story just as in yours and mine.

Every once in a while our lives need to be cleared of clutter. It's like me sorting out my sock drawer on the day after Christmas. I took out the top layer of socks and attempted to match a few sets. I soon gave up. I had received four pairs of socks for Christmas, which made matters worse. I concluded the most intelligent thing to do was to dump the drawer and start all over with new socks.

The clutter that fills our lives is the same. There comes a time when the spiritual sock drawer needs dumping. Then God can fill it again.

All dreamers go through a periodic stripping away — little pieces of unfinished business that need clearing up, a feeling of guilt about something here, an unconfessed sin over there. A good pit helps the cleaning process.

OVERCOMMITMENT: A DREAM KILLER

Overcommitment is a perfect example of our need to be stripped down in the pit. Overcommitment is really an attempt to be more than what we are.

I once preached a sermon attempting to highlight the damage done by overcommitment. I brought an over-stuffed suitcase — with pant legs sticking out of the side and the lock beginning to break — and threw it on the platform.

"Does this look like anybody's life," I asked, "overcommitted and overstuffed?"

Laughter filled the sanctuary. Everyone knew that suitcase was an exact picture of most of our lives. Then I opened the suitcase, brought in a garbage can and disposed of the excess baggage.

Few of us will ever get rid of our excess on our own, so God sends along a pit so that we get our coats stolen. The good news is that reducing clutter can speed a dreamer on to completion.

Why is it so important that we lose our coats? The key is not in the coat but in what it symbolizes. I once visited an inmate on death row who killed a young man for his leather jacket. To him, that coat symbolized prestige, acceptance and wealth. The coats in our lives may represent many things, but at one time or another all true dreamers get stripped down to nothing.

When we started our church on the east side of Seattle, I left a prestigious position in a growing church in central Washington. In addition, I had been enrolled in a doctoral program that would allow time to be a leader at a burgeoning Bible college.

One of my friends flew all the way from Florida to try to talk me out of the move. Yet I knew that God was calling us to begin with nothing.

Those were powerful days. Our church was only ten people meeting in our living room. We couldn't afford to rent the house we lived in, so we made a six-month agreement with the landlord to paint, repair the house, clean the pool and relandscape the yard. We literally had nothing.

My wife and I were talking the other night about how fearful those days were. My wife felt very alone and frightened, and so did I. The two of us never talked about it until twelve years later. But we had to agree it allowed the Lord to work a dream through us that we could only partly imagine.

We have a woman in our church named Marcia Jones who sings and plays the guitar. She also has a disease called lupus, which causes tremendous pain in the joints of her fingers. As a recording artist, she has produced two tapes. If you didn't know her, I don't think you would know the beauty of the music she plays. She plays in pain. Her disease often strips her down to nothing but her reliance upon God. Marcia is a true dreamer. She has been in the pit and lost her coat, but she has kept the essence of her dream.

DREAMERS PAY THEIR OWN WAY

Those of us who are dreamers often try to help those who follow after us to avoid the pain we have experienced, so we create weak followers. I certainly wouldn't want many of the people I am mentoring to feel the pain I have felt. But as I study the life of Joseph, I realize that every dreamer must go through a pit of his own.

Rocky Bleier, a college student with a promising career in football, fell into a pit. His leg was injured in the Vietnam War. Yet he returned, against all odds, and became a Superbowl running back for the Pittsburgh Steelers. He now commands a healthy speaking salary and teaches others how to have the guts to come back from the pits.

O. J. Simpson had bowed legs as a child. His mother taped boards to each side of his legs until they straightened out. O. J. went on to run in the NFL as few others have.

These are great, motivational stories. But the truth is, not everyone who goes to the pit comes away running like O. J. Simpson or Rocky Bleier. They went to the pit and walked away empty-handed. Yet they are still dreamers.

The struggle makes the dream all that much sweeter. I believe that Joseph, as an old man, would have passed by a fancy coat. God had a different coat for him, and he knew it. Like his Lord, his back was covered by the scars of a slave.

WE ALL FEAR LOSS

I am told that most people have a dream such as I have had on occasion. I dream that I show up to preach wearing nothing but my boxers. I had a similar version of this dream when I was in college. There I would be, sitting in class in my underwear. Everyone would be pointing and laughing.

I've wondered aloud in my dreams how I could have gotten up in the pulpit without anyone noticing. Surely one of my friends would have helped me.

A counseling friend of mine says this particular dream betrays the fear we all have of self-disclosure. It began in the garden when Adam and Eve's first reaction to their nakedness was to hide and wrap fig leaves around themselves. This fear drives us to run to symbols. God continually has to strip away these symbols: titles, gimmicks, insurance policies that protect us from failure.

My graduation from college was less than a triumphal event. I had my coat yanked from me in front of the world.

Several days before the celebration at the Seattle Opera House, I went to the bookstore at Seattle Pacific University. To my surprise I was listed as having graduated *magna cum laude*. If you have this honor, you get to wear two gold cords around your shoulders. This signifies that you aren't just above average, but that you are a bit above that. Of course, above this level is graduating *summa cum laude*. We don't like to talk about those people.

I was surprised that I was on this list. By my calculations I should have only graduated *cum laude*, with something like a 3.6 grade point average. Graduating *magna cum laude* required a 3.75 grade point average. I had received several C grades when I was a freshman in junior college. So by my calculations I didn't fit the profile of a *magna cum laude* graduate.

Nonetheless, I took the cords with glee and thought I had made the mistake. I hurried home to tell my wife that I was graduating *magna cum laude*. I even called my parents.

Approximately five hundred of us graduated that year. As the ceremonies began that night we were all lined up in the halls outside the large auditorium. Then the dean of education (who will remain nameless) walked by. He noticed that I was wearing two honor cords.

He looked at me a bit puzzled as he passed. I didn't think much of it. But then he walked by again with his secretary. "Murren," he said, "you shouldn't be wearing two tassles."

"Doctor," I said, "the bookstore had me listed as *magna cum laude*. I also had these two tassles in my graduation packet with my cap and gown. I paid for them. As far as I know, the orders came from your office."

He marched me to a little side room where they had a computer set up to make certain that no one slipped through his purview who had unpaid bills or maybe missed a class or something.

Sure enough, the bookstore had made a mistake. I was only to graduate *cum laude*. About a dozen of my friends had been quite impressed with my earlier status. Now I was sent back with only one cord. I was busted.

I had traveled long enough with the Lord by then to thank Him all the way back. To tell you the truth, I was tempted to take the other cord off, figuring that if I was to learn humility, then I would strip down to nothing.

I have often laughed about that situation over the years. Jesus warned about taking the front seat. He said to take the backseat and let Him call you forward.

God loves to teach us to leave behind the symbols for the real thing. Our fear of nakedness causes us to cover ourselves with symbols. At the same time we hide our need for Christ.

One man in the history of the United States was able to cover his own nakedness. He was James Michael Curley, once the mayor of Boston. Around the turn of the century he was imprisoned for embezzlement. While in prison he was elected governor of Massachusetts. Once elected, he commuted his own sentence and absolved his guilt.

Now James Curley may have been able to do that, but we can't do that for ourselves. We require God's covering. Joseph was learning that God wanted to be his covering. God wanted to be his coat, the only sign of his inheritance.

Yes, one of our greatest dream-stoppers is our reluctance to be stripped down to reliance upon God. Our attachment to symbols keeps us from the real thing. Keeping your dreams will entail thanking God for the pit.

LIFE APPLICATION

- Have you ever lost a symbol that was important to you? Are you willing to accept the fact that maybe God was behind it?

- Have you ever lost an opportunity to minister? Perhaps you were replaced by another and were humiliated by it? That is actually a great occasion for you to praise God. You are being stripped down so that your dream will grow.

PRAYER

Lord, thank You that You allow us to fall into pits so that we are stripped of symbols we don't need. Thank You for being the source of all our dreams, the One who spoke all the worlds into existence, the One who saw us naked and gave His life as a covering.

NINE

NO SOLITARY DREAMERS

The Lord was with Joseph and he prospered, and he lived in the house of his Egyptian master (Gen. 39:2, italics added).

But while Joseph was there in prison, *the Lord was with him*; he showed him kindness and granted him favor in the eyes of the prison warden (Gen. 39:20b-21, italics added).

The Lord was with Joseph and gave him success in whatever he did (Gen. 39:23b, italics added).

So Pharaoh asked them, "Can we find anyone

like this man, *one in whom is the spirit of God?"*
(Gen. 41:38, italics added).

SCENE: *Palace dining room of Joseph the governor, 1682 B.C.*

JOSEPH: The pain was so intense today, God of my fathers. Lord, how good to be reunited with my brothers. The agony of the separation filled my heart, but within seconds my heart became aware also that I never really had been alone.

You truly are the ladder to heaven that my father, Jacob, often told me about. I know now why that was so real to him. Dreamers are never alone!

Oh, how my heart beat when all my brothers bowed to me, as my dream said they would. But what a different meaning it had for me. I didn't feel superior at all. I was their servant as they all bowed.

How many years ago I had that dream, and yet how wonderful that I have never felt alone. Separated, yes. Agonizingly living on memories, certainly. But I have learned to focus my eyes on You, the Dream Giver. And now, as my brothers bow to me, I bow to You.

DREAMS EXPLODE ON THE SCENE

The other day I was driving down the road in my four-wheel-drive pickup truck. I love to drink Squirt soft drinks. I was particularly thirsty that day. I don't know why, but I was shaking the bottle around absentmindedly. I guess I like to stir up the little chunks of lemon in the pop. Usually I let it sit still for a few minutes before I open it.

This day something was on my mind. I can't remember

what it was — something to do with my kids. You know how they can captivate your mind. So, without thinking, I twisted the cap off the glass bottle. Ka-blew-ee! Pop blew everywhere, nearly hitting the ceiling, filling my lap and shooting over into the passenger seat, leaving a small puddle.

I think dreams work this way. God bottles them up in our hearts like carbonated pop. Then life has a way of rattling and shaking them, with all its twists and turns, until one day the cap comes off. I know dreams in my life have seemed to work this way. When you have just about given up on them, they don't just eke onto the scene. They explode.

I thought of this while meditating on Joseph's reunion with his brothers.

> Now Joseph was the governor of the land, the one who sold grain to all its people. So when Joseph's brothers arrived, they bowed down to him with their faces to the ground. As soon as Joseph saw his brothers, he recognized them... (Gen. 42:6-7).

Imagine how Joseph must have felt. He had been perplexed by the dream of his youth, knowing it had been real, but not understanding how it could ever be fulfilled. Then all at once it exploded onto the scene like a shaken-up soda pop.

Joseph knew what was happening when his dream burst onto the scene because he'd had a partner all along the way. No one dreams alone. If we walk with the Dream Giver, the fulfillment of our dreams won't take us off guard either.

David (formerly Paul) Yonggi Cho, pastor of the world's largest church, has a now-famous illustration of how faith works. He says, "When one has faith, it's like being pregnant." He tells a wonderful story of how he asked the

Lord to give him a bicycle, a desk and a typewriter, and how the Lord assured him he would receive it. He says the Lord told him to be "pregnant with the seed of the promise."

Dreams work like faith. You become pregnant with a dream, just as a mother becomes pregnant with a child. Then it bursts onto the scene when the time for delivery is right.

I remember when our daughter was born. I was preparing to go to Russia to visit some Jewish friends I had met while in Warsaw, Poland. Two nights before I was due to leave, Deb woke me up at 2:00 A.M. hemorrhaging. Her labor had begun suddenly with a tear in the internal lining of her womb.

I got dressed hurriedly, phoned the doctor, packed her in our Mazda RX2 and sped to the hospital. When we arrived, the doors were locked. At first I contemplated driving my car through the glass-plated doors. However, I managed to control myself and screamed at the top of my lungs instead, "Let me in! Let me in!" It seemed like days, but I'm sure it was just minutes before the hospital attendant came and opened the door.

I blurted out, "My wife is pregnant, and she's bleeding intensely! The doctor is on his way." The attendant grabbed a wheelchair. We both placed her gently in it and hurried her into the emergency room. Within half an hour, two doctors met me in the hospital lobby to confer on a decision they were having to make.

The doctor said, "We can either take the baby too fast and certainly kill it, or we can let the process continue and run the certain risk that your wife will bleed to death before we can stop the hemorrhaging."

Before the words could fully work through the neurons in my brain, we heard a baby's cry from the other room. Raissa had been born.

We had known there was a baby in Deb's womb. We even had a fair idea of what she would be like, being a combination of the gene pool of the Murrens and Landins.

But once she burst onto the scene, we knew exactly what she was like.

Dreams can happen suddenly, too, yet they are sometimes preceded by a high level of uncertainty. I felt very alone in the hospital when Raissa was born — all alone facing the possible death of my wife or my new child. Yet with the doctors there, I was comforted. They had been through this before. They seemed confident they could handle the job. I've found that it's much easier to wait for the birth of a dream when you're standing with an Expert.

NO ONE DREAMS ALONE

It's obvious that dreamers need to keep their eyes on God while they pursue the fulfillment of their dreams. But does God want dreamers to isolate themselves from other people?

You and I have both met the type — people who feel they have dreams so superior that they can't fit into others' lives. This is not the spirit of an authentic dream from God.

Ephesians 4 talks about the body of Christ being knit together. God provides each wonderful gift that fits in and makes the whole picture. The appeal of the chapter is for unity among empowered people who make up God's dreams.

On the other hand, some solitude is needed. One of my favorite books is *Life Together* by Dietrich Bonhoeffer, a German theologian who was martyred by the Nazis in 1945. In this book he wrote about the life of solitude and the Christian community. He contended that a healthy spiritual life has times of aloneness with God and times of community with God's people.

I happen to love solitude. For me, community is a discipline. For many of my friends, it's the opposite — solitude is a discipline. They are more extroverted and love being with people. No matter what our temperaments, solitude will help us be healthy dreamers.

None of the Bible's great dreamers really had a sense of isolation while in their solitude. I think Jesus was affirming this when He said, "[The Father] will give you another Counselor to be with you forever" (John 14:16).

Over and over in the story of Joseph, we read, "The Lord was with Joseph" (Gen. 39:2).

But feelings of isolation or deep pain when alone are signs of depression. These feelings can also be signs of separation from God because of unresolved sins.

From reading the book of Psalms, I've concluded David experienced both situations. He had times of deep depression caused by situational problems and, possibly, by a genetic predisposition to depression. David also mourned about separation from God when he knew he was hiding sin in his heart. If being alone causes you pain, ask God to show you the cause and what you should do about it.

Our solitary times are not times of isolation and aloneness. They are times of partnership when we draw aside and let the Dream Giver define the meaning of our dreams. Then the call comes to unite with all dreamers. Encouraging and networking with one another, we become like one beautifully tuned orchestra.

20/20 HINDSIGHT

No one dreams alone, but at times our awareness that we are not alone is discovered by 20/20 hindsight.

About seven years ago our church faced such extreme growth that the county officials were putting pressure on us to relocate. However, we really didn't have the funds to move.

Our neighbors were organizing ad hoc meetings. They were upset with the traffic that filled the small streets around our facility. And they didn't want us buying any more houses in the neighborhood to convert into children's church space.

The circumstances sent a clear message: It was time to move. Over a six-month period we prayed and felt the assurance that God was leading us, but there was no sign of any open doors.

One morning in a local café in a small community near our church, one of the men assisting me in the search for a new site was having coffee. He overheard a group of Catholic businessmen commenting that the new site for their building project had been turned down by the archbishop.

The conversation caught my friend's ears, so he asked to sit in. He found the location of the site, got a feel for its approximate cost and gave me a call that morning.

Within two days we were sitting in the office of the archbishop's land representative. We proposed that they sell the property to us, since they were not going to build on the site. At that time the property consisted of ten acres. Within months we would also be able to purchase the ten acres next door to the property.

To our great surprise, the price matched our ability to pay. To raise the funds, we had help from our denominational leaders, and a number of church members pooled their resources. We were able to purchase the property at a price that had been placed in escrow four or five years earlier.

I'll never forget the excitement in my heart when I knew for sure God was leading our move. I had been frightened of my own ambition. I always feared that I wanted to lead a large church so I could say I'd done it. I worried about using people to fulfill some sort of aspiration of my own.

But we knew without a doubt that God was leading us this time. The exciting part for me was the awareness after the fact that God had been with us all along. I think that's the way it usually works. While we're waiting for dreams to come to pass, we know He's there, but then again we don't know. Don't be surprised if the awareness of God's partnership in your dreaming follows your commitment to that dream in dark and lonely times.

THE FAMILIAR STRANGER

Now that same day two of them were going to a village called Emmaus, about seven miles from Jerusalem. They were talking with each other about everything that had happened. As they talked and discussed these things with each other, Jesus himself came up and walked along with them; but they were kept from recognizing him.

He asked them, "What are you discussing together as you walk along?"

They stood still, their faces downcast. One of them, named Cleopas, asked him, "Are you only a visitor to Jerusalem and do not know the things that have happened there in these days?"

"What things?" he asked.

"About Jesus of Nazareth," they replied. "He was a prophet, powerful in word and deed before God and all the people. The chief priests and our rulers handed him over to be sentenced to death, and they crucified him; but we had hoped that he was the one who was going to redeem Israel. And what is more, it is the third day since all this took place. In addition, some of our women amazed us. They went to the tomb early this morning but didn't find his body. They came and told us that they had seen a vision of angels, who said he was alive. Then some of our companions went to the tomb and found it just as the women had said, but him they did not see."

He said to them, "How foolish you are, and

how slow of heart to believe all that the prophets have spoken! Did not the Christ have to suffer these things and then enter his glory?" And beginning with Moses and all the Prophets, he explained to them what was said in all the Scriptures concerning himself.

As they approached the village to which they were going, Jesus acted as if he were going farther. But they urged him strongly, "Stay with us, for it is nearly evening; the day is almost over." So he went in to stay with them.

When he was at the table with them, he took bread, gave thanks, broke it and began to give it to them. Then their eyes were opened and they recognized him, and he disappeared from their sight. They asked each other, "Were not our hearts burning within us while he talked with us on the road and opened the Scriptures to us?"

They got up and returned at once to Jerusalem. There they found the Eleven and those with them, assembled together and saying, "It is true! The Lord has risen and has appeared to Simon." Then the two told what had happened on the way, and how Jesus was recognized by them when he broke the bread (Luke 24:13-35).

Like the two disciples on the road to Emmaus, often we don't recognize our Partner. But like the disciples, we always have a Familiar Stranger accompanying us.

Remember, these fellows had given at least three years of their lives to the cause. They had been ridiculed for aligning themselves with the dreams of this Messiah. This Jesus of Nazareth had said He would change the world, and now He was crucified. Their plans were shattered, their vision of a Roman-free Israel was gone, and the wonderful joy of living in the presence of the great Teacher was snatched from them.

What hope lay ahead for them? Nothing. They were headed home.

We, like those disciples, need our eyes opened on a regular basis to be able to see Jesus all around us. And we, like the disciples, will be questioned. In this beautiful section of Scripture, we are awakened to several great truths.

- Jesus walked with His disciples (v. 15). This is a template reminder for us that we don't walk alone.

- He asked them (v. 17). Christ, the great question-asker, uses the everyday challenges of life to ask His probing questions. Are we committed to the dream? Can we trust God to the fullest?

- He explained (v. 27). Christ's presence sometimes is the only explanation for life. I have a friend who has lived with excruciating pain for ten years. He asked me why God was letting him suffer. I was quiet for several minutes, feeling deep compassion for the suffering he had gone through and searching for a genuine answer. Finally I turned to him and said, "The only explanation I know is that this world is imperfect, out of sync and out of alignment. But Christ has chosen to walk with us in this world."

- He stayed with them (v. 29). Our Familiar Stranger is willing to go wherever we go. The address of our house is of no importance to Him, neither is our vocation. He has chosen to be with us. Like the early disciples, our first call is to be with Him before we are called to do anything else.

- He ate with them (v. 30). In the Bible, eating is the ultimate statement of fellowship and friendship. This goes far beyond simple communion or even the great *agape* love described in 1 Corinthians 13. To eat with us means that God chooses to imbibe deeply in the give-and-take and ordinary hustle and bustle of our lives.

- He disappeared after they could see (v. 31). God has a way of doing that. He leads us to the point of discovery, fully discloses Himself and then steps back to allow us, with 20/20 hindsight, to see that we were never alone.

THE PROP MAN RETURNS

When I was about ten years old, my friend Randy Rich and I decided we would go camping by ourselves. At first our parents were reluctant to turn two ten-year-olds loose in the mountains.

There is a Boy Scout camp just southwest of Wenatchee, Washington, where he and I grew up. It had lots of campsites that were close to civilization, yet they were far enough away to let you know you were in the woods. Growing up in the area as a Boy Scout, I had been exposed to the local folklore about some of the creatures that inhabited the hillsides around the area.

The chief figure of the local folklore was a fellow called the Prop Man. The Prop Man was dead but alive. There had been a plane crash during World War II in the hillsides around this camp. As the story went, the pilot still roamed the hillsides with a prop through his torso. He had been spotted through multiple generations, and he was likely to lunge out from behind clumps of trees on unsuspecting campers at any time.

Randy and I were dropped off by our parents a short distance from the campsite of our choice, which was near the mythic terrain of the Prop Man. We pitched our tent, prepared the camp and then took a hike. By the time we returned, dusk had fallen.

We built a fire and cooked our pork and beans in the can over the flames. (If you and a fellow ten-year-old have never eaten beans this way, you have missed out on the finest of cuisine.) Then we roasted marshmallows and finally ended our meal with burnt hotdogs and scorched buns. As darkness slipped in around us, we flipped on our radio and started listening to a local baseball game.

Somehow our conversation turned to the Prop Man. Randy assured me that there had been three or four authentic sightings in the last ten years or so. I wanted to be skeptical, but I was a total believer.

As the fire dimmed, the night became pitch-black. It was the kind of black that only happens in the middle of the woods at night. It slips over the faces of unsuspecting boys and stuffs up their throats so they are unable to catch their breath.

When this kind of night fell, we retreated to our tent, turned on our lantern and continued to talk. We tried a number of conversations, but neither of us could get our minds off the Prop Man.

As Randy reached up to turn off the light, I was happy. I was ready to go to sleep. I figured it was the only solace from the Prop Man. We both lay there silently. Neither of us was breathing the kind of deep-sleep breathing that should happen. I could only hear the rapid, shallow breathing of four little lungs trying to get enough oxygen to maintain life. After all, the Prop Man could lunge through the tent door at any moment.

Agonizingly we both drifted off to sleep. Aaah, safe at last. But then it happened! We both heard it. We could feel the ground shaking. *Pound, pound, pound, thump, thump, thump.* We could hear it come through the bushes.

I nearly screamed but held it in. After all, we were safe

in our tent. I sat up as Randy sat up. I am sure to this day that I could see the whites of his eyes through the dark. I am certain that he could see mine too.

"What is that?" he whispered.

"I don't know," I replied. Neither of us would mention the Prop Man.

The pounding footsteps tromped through our campsite, circled around once and left. We both lay motionless for ten minutes or more.

That night every brush of the tree branches awakened me. I was so tired by morning that I could have slept for three days.

We were both up at first light, back over our fireplace, scrambling eggs, cooking bacon, hurriedly cleaning up around camp. We kept our noses to the ground, looking for footprints.

"Do you suppose it was a bear?" Randy finally asked.

"I don't know," I said, "but whatever it was, we must have scared it off." We both knew that we were lying to each other.

That evening our mothers picked us up, ending a great weekend in the woods. I must say that we were both quite excited not to spend another night out there. After all, we had survived the Prop Man's visit once. We couldn't gamble on a second visit.

As we loaded our gear in the car, my mom turned to me with a big smile. "Good to see you fellows. How did it go?"

"Oh, it was tremendous! The food was good, and we had a great hike in the mountains," I said.

"Doug, you look terribly tired," she answered. "How did you sleep?"

We both chimed in together, "We slept real good."

Before we could tell her about the Prop Man visit, she said, "Did you see George Weeks? Did he stop and say hi?"

We turned and looked across the backseat at each other. "Why?" we asked simultaneously.

My mom filled us in. "He said he was going to go up to

the camp around dusk to make sure that you fellows were OK. Did he ever show up?"

We both breathed a sigh of relief. Instead of the Prop Man being out to get us, it was in fact our local forest ranger, coming out to ensure that all was well.

This story is a wonderful illustration of how we often respond to the Lord's presence. Our fears often distort our ability to see Him with us in our dreaming. Our fears often keep us from seeing Him at all. In fact, we confuse Him for the Prop Man.

One time Jesus walked on water to meet His disciples (Mark 6:45-56). The Bible says that when evening came, the boat was in the middle of the lake. Yet Christ had been left on shore. A storm blew in, and the disciples grabbed the oars, but they were not getting anywhere. About the fourth watch of the night Jesus came out walking on the lake. He just about walked right past the disciples in their boat. But when they saw Him walking on the lake, they thought He was a ghost. They began screaming and jumping around in the boat.

They cried out because they didn't recognize Jesus in the middle of their storms.

We, like them, so easily forget that He is present even in our storms. When our dreams are being shaken about, we confuse the figure beside us for the Prop Man or a ghost in the night when it is our ever-present Friend.

So don't consider yourself unusual if you're fearful in the middle of your dream. Train your eyes to view His work through a new paradigm. If you believe that God only works when things are going well, if you think that God only works when there is great provision available, if you think that God only works when there is relational harmony, you will not see God in the middle of much of His workings in your life.

LIFE APPLICATION

As we have seen, no dreamer dreams alone.

What makes God-given dreams so powerful is the company that He gives us along the way. It isn't the smallness or bigness of the dream that makes the difference. The powerful presence of the Holy Spirit and interlocking fellowship with other dreamers in the body of Christ assures us of safety and triumph. Here are some key points to remember.

- Count on the sudden, serendipitous outworking of your dream, which will give you 20/20 hindsight vision. Look back and rejoice that God has been with you all along.

- When you enter into a dream, remember that it isn't the spectacular nature of the dream that makes it God-given. It is the fact that He has chosen to be with you.

- When you begin dreaming, realize that with the dream comes the promise of His company.

- When separated, remind yourself that you are not alone.

- Let him into the boat of your life when the storms are raging. Learn to recognize Him in adverse circumstances.

- Build a network of friends and fellow dreamers.

- Are you looking at the dream more than the Dream Giver? If so, you may be asking for trouble. Why don't you pause and ask Christ by the Holy Spirit to make the Dream Giver bigger in your heart than the dream you have received? You'll enjoy the journey much more.

TEN

FORGIVENESS: NECESSARY EQUIPMENT OF A BELIEVER

The chief cupbearer, however, did not remember Joseph; he forgot him (Gen. 40:23).

When Joseph's brothers saw that their father was dead, they said, "What if Joseph holds a grudge against us and pays us back for all the wrongs we did to him?" (Gen. 50:15).

But Joseph said to them, "Don't be afraid. Am I in the place of God? You intended to harm me, but God intended it for good to accomplish what is now being done, the saving of many lives. So then, don't be afraid...." And he reassured them and spoke kindly to them (Gen. 50:19).

I have found that to experience all that God has for me, I need an ever-growing life perspective that is big enough to contain God's plans. I have also found that with a growing perspective I need a growing heart. The sign of a growing heart is a spirit of forgiveness.

SCENE: *Joseph's palace, memorial room for Jacob, 1659 B.C.*

JOSEPH: Father, my heart is broken as I see your body lie there and I sense the fears in my brothers. I can see they do not realize the great work that God has done in my heart. They meant to work evil against me. But I have learned that your great God, the God of Abraham and Isaac, was even in all the misdeeds. How can I hold a grudge against those whom God has used? Their wrongdoing, after all, has been the making of my heart.

I have forgiven Potiphar. He knew that his wife was making up a tale, that I would never consider assaulting her. He came and spoke to me one night in the prison, asking me to forgive him, telling me that he didn't know what else to do. He couldn't afford to lose his honor. I remember clutching the bars, leaning up against them, telling him what a good master he had been. I was surprised when I forgave him and his wife. Then I languished in prison for two years, forgotten. I interpreted a dream for the king's cupbearer. He was freed. I remained incarcerated. He forgot me.

Later the same man clutched my coat and asked me to explain Pharaoh's dream. Then he asked for my forgiveness. I forgave him, and my heart grew.

The dreams of God cannot be halted, but the hearts of men can shrink too small to contain them. The wise old grandfather of Pharaoh spoke those words to me one afternoon. As I prayed to the God of Abraham, Isaac and Jacob, I began to see His divine hand in timing the most ill-intended and ill-fated events in my life. I have decided that great men forgive.

I can only pray that my brothers will believe me when I say this, and even forgive themselves.

During my college days I loved to fish. When I lived at home, I pilfered my dad's fishing equipment. He had plenty of flies and bait.

Once I moved from home, I was dependent on my own equipment. One of my friends, Gordon, used to hate to go fishing with me. The reason was that I never showed up with enough equipment to do the task. I would borrow his best flies and lose them.

Finally one day he said, "Murren, if you are going to fish, you have to get the right equipment. If you show up next time without the right gear, we are through fishing. Got it?"

By the next fishing trip I had bought the right bait and plenty of flies. I even had enough to share.

Sometimes I have also shown up without the right equipment to handle God's dreams in my life. Most often lacking is a forgiving spirit.

Christ told His disciples that in His kingdom you needed to forgive your brother seventy times seven times a day (Matt. 18:22). The idea of the passage was that forgiveness was an unending exercise for those who share in God's kingdom. One could never forgive enough when dealing with humans.

I have always been humored by the disciples' next appeal: "Lord, increase our faith!" (Luke 17:5). A sure sign of great faith is a great ability to forgive. As Peter observed later, "Love covers over a multitude of sins" (1 Pet. 4:8). It takes great faith to have great love. If one has great dreams for children, he or she had better be prepared to have great forgiveness. The dream of a great marriage must also be powered by an ability to forgive.

One wonders how many dreams are locked up in the prison of unforgiveness? Joseph's heart was always free because he was able to forgive.

I recently assisted in the recovery of a pastor who had fallen into an affair with a woman in his church. I suspected that at the root of his affair was anger with his church. "Is there anything about your church that would have gotten you so angry as to be vulnerable to such a thing?" I asked him.

His response was quick and strong: "First, they never supported any of our building expansions. And several people left the church when I wanted to move into a new worship direction. Then when I felt the Lord leading us into free-flowing gifts of healing, they wouldn't go with me."

Sensing he was also in a state of depression, I proceeded with great care to tell him that I saw his behavior as a symptom of a deep-seated disillusionment with himself and an inability to forgive himself as a leader. I suggested he possibly also had some deeper problems that would require professional care. His first step was to unlock the door to forgiveness, releasing himself and others. We prayed a prayer of forgiveness so that his dreams could return.

ARE YOU WILLING TO PAY THE PRICE?

There is an old Russian fable that Mary, the mother of

Jesus, wasn't the first young virgin that heaven attempted to recruit. As the story goes, the angel Gabriel traveled about the land of Judah from house to house, looking for a virgin willing to pay the price of misunderstanding and the agony of being the mother of the Savior of the world.

As the fable concludes, Mary was the first and only one of the virgins who would accept the burden of such an assignment. Her betrothed, Joseph, also paid the price of misunderstanding and unfair accusation. For me and most leaders who concentrate on maintaining the highest level of integrity possible, the greatest insult is to be falsely accused.

When Joseph was a servant in Potiphar's house, he was blasted cruelly by false accusation of sexual harassment. This was particularly painful for him because he had been loyal to his master in all things.

It is interesting that after he became ruler of the land, there is no record of retaliation on Potiphar's house. Joseph accepted the price of dreaming.

WHAT IS FORGIVENESS?

Many people don't understand what forgiveness is. Conducting multitudes of marriage counseling sessions has accentuated my awareness of severe misunderstandings regarding the Christian experience of forgiveness. Let's sketch quickly what we mean by forgiveness.

Forgiveness is the willingness to:

- see someone as more than their sins.

- give up the right to retaliate.

- acknowledge your sin first.

- bless and hope for a better and brighter future for the violator.

- not rehearse or bring up again the sin with others.

- pray for God's will to be fulfilled in the violator.

The word *forgiveness* means "to send away." The Old Testament scapegoat is a wonderful picture of the exercise of a forgiving heart. In the Old Testament the Israelites were instructed to make atonement each year, using two goats. One goat was sacrificed. The high priest laid his hands on the other goat and confessed all the sins of the people over it. The goat was then released into the desert to wander until its death. The idea was that the sins were forever forgotten. The psalmist would later word it this way: "As far as the east is from the west, so far has he removed our transgressions from us" (Ps. 103:12).

WHAT FORGIVENESS ISN'T

As well as needing to have a positive definition of forgiveness, we need to have clear in our minds what it is not.

- Forgiveness is *not* the ability to forget. Emotional pain and injury may be strongly etched in our minds. You will recall times of pain. It is what you choose to do with those memories that makes you a forgiver or an unforgiver.

- Forgiveness is *not* the willingness to be subjected to abuse. In some cases you need to forgive and leave the abusive situation at the same time.

- Forgiveness is *not* good feelings about the person or situation. In fact, you may feel bad — and should feel bad — when harmed.

- Forgiveness is *not* the willingness to overlook the matter and not talk about it. Confrontation is necessary for true forgiveness, repentance and healing to occur in a relationship.

FORGIVING YOURSELF

The hardest person for you to forgive is yourself. I wouldn't be surprised if Joseph spent many a night wishing he'd been more tactful with the sharing of his dreams.

Larry was from the South and a terrific guitar player. He had a definite call on his life. Being raised in a Pentecostal home, he had learned to pray in the Spirit as a youngster. But when he was eighteen, he took his guitar and toured with a rock and roll band around the United States. He later renounced that life-style and rededicated his life to God.

I met him when he was in his late twenties. He was convinced that God would never be able to use him again. It was evident to all of his friends, however, that he had a great talent for songwriting that could really spread the gospel.

"When one turns away from the Lord, it's impossible to come back to your original anointing," he lectured us one night. "Don't you guys fall away. Don't you do what I did, or you'll never again be able to enter back into what you once had." I could tell he believed what he was saying. In my heart I thought, Phooey. This is nonsense.

God is the God of the second chance. I've learned over the years that one of the enemy's greatest tactics against would-be dreamers is to remind them constantly of their failings and shortcomings. His aim is to convince them that once a dream has been aborted, damaged or crippled, it can never be restored.

I think of Larry from time to time. I think of the lie he believed. I haven't seen him for years, but I do hope that his dream has been unlocked from the prison of self-unforgiveness.

In our congregation we make a habit of not having any paid pastor do the baptizing. Everyone who is baptized is baptized by either a lay pastor or the friend who led him to Christ.

Several years ago, however, I decided I wanted to do the baptism one Sunday morning when I wasn't preaching. A young woman named Cathy was being baptized along with several others.

On this occasion I uncharacteristically took time to interview briefly the people who had come to be baptized — as we stood in the water. In front of more than a thousand people Cathy said that she had attended our church for two years before she had received Christ.

Everybody got a big laugh out of the fact that she had actually come to the Lord when my assistant was preaching — this, after hearing me preach for nearly two years.

After the baptismal part of the service, I waited outside the changing area. I wanted to ask Cathy some questions.

She was surprised when she saw me waiting. As I sat on the steps by the prayer room, I asked if she had a minute to talk. "Cathy," I continued, "why is it that you sat in our church for two years before you received Christ?"

"It took me that long to believe you would really love me," she answered. "You see, I was raised in a Christian home, and I fell away from the Lord. I've had three abortions. Some of my friends said this was the church to go to, that you would really love me. But I just couldn't believe it."

"Would you believe that God would want you to share that love with others?"

A beaming smile spread across her face. "I certainly would," she said. "I want to tell them that there really is deep love and God really does forgive. He really can bring you back to where you once were."

"It's always exciting to see dreamers return to their

vision," I assured her, "after being locked up in unforgiveness."

LIFE APPLICATION

- Have you ever been abused or mistreated? I'm certain you have. Are you able, right now where you are, to thank God in the misunderstanding and abuse?

- Have you expressed the wrong kind of forgiveness or remained in an abusive situation? If so, seek professional help. Get some advice. You are never called by God to be destroyed at the hands of an abuser.

- Are you able to forgive yourself? Do you believe that you can return to your dreams once you have fallen? The way back is always repentance, which simply means turning back in the right direction. I encourage all would-be dreamers who have lost their dreams because of unforgiveness — either of self or others — to discover the beauty of a growing heart.

Yes, forgiveness is necessary equipment for all would-be dreamers. The greater the dream, the greater the need for forgiveness will arise. The more impact your ministry and dream will have on others, the more misunderstood you'll be. This can cause a life to bend under the force of those winds at times. But great dreamers, like Joseph, learn to forgive. The exercise of forgiveness makes for large hearts, big enough for God's dreams.

ELEVEN

THE DREAM SEDUCERS

Now Joseph was well-built and handsome, and after a while his master's wife took notice of Joseph and said, "Come to bed with me!" But he refused (Gen. 39:6b-8a).

And though she spoke to Joseph day after day, he refused to go to bed with her or even be with her (Gen. 39:10).

SCENE: *The sleeping chambers of Potiphar's wife, 1692 B.C.*

POTIPHAR'S
WIFE: Why did he flee? Am I losing my beauty?

Why wouldn't such a man succumb to my seductions?

I will not be rejected. I must act quickly, though. I know he will go tell old Potiphar.

The boy has avoided me for months. Maybe he already talked to Potiphar!

But now he's fleeing through the streets without a cloak. Someone will know something is wrong. I can do something before he tells.

(Shouting) Guards! Guards! I've been attacked by the Hebrew boy! Call my husband, quickly. I've been attacked!

(Quietly) What is in the heart of such a man who would resist temptation so strongly? Such a strange man. An eerie man. I find him frightening in his strength.

THE TEMPTATION FACTOR

Well, now, Joseph has lost his second coat (Gen. 39:12). This time it was wrenched away from him by a dream seducer. Joseph showed a character of steel as he faced sexual temptation day in and day out. We mustn't forget he would have been in his late teens or early twenties and at the peak of his sexual development, according to psychologists of our time. Entrusted with a great deal of power, he no doubt had great opportunities for secrecy.

Temptation serves a great purpose in God's master plan for our lives. If we don't understand it, we can become either fearful or lax in facing the challenges to our character that would lead us off the path.

There are four things that can be accomplished in a dreamer's life only through temptation.

- *Temptation builds character.*
That's right. Find your area of temptation, and you find

the edge of your personal spiritual development. Don't sweat it if what you see isn't all that pretty. That's a good discovery in and of itself. I'm convinced that our doubts and our temptations show us the frontier of our spiritual growth. As James writes:

> Consider it pure joy, my brothers, whenever you face trials of many kinds, because you know that the testing of your faith develops perseverance. Perseverance must finish its work so that you may be mature and complete, not lacking anything (1:2-3).

Without temptation we can't note our progress, neither can we be aware of our real dangers.

- *Temptation adds pressure that forces us to God.*

Most of us are lazy. Few of us live to our potential. One of my friends says the phrase "He has great potential" actually means, "He could really do something, but he's not doing much, is he?"

I find temptation forces me to draw nearer to God. It's no longer a matter of having the *potential* of intimacy with God. I cry out to Him because I need Him.

- *Temptation gives us insight for future battles.*

Battles of the past are building blocks preparing us to stand under greater temptation.

LIES ABOUT TEMPTATION

We all believe lies, but some lies are more deadly than others. The tooth fairy is based on a myth, but she doesn't cause many problems. However, if you believe the myth that it's OK to drive into a wall at eighty miles an hour — that would be a deadly lie.

Let's look at seven lies about temptation that can trip

up would-be dreamers.

- If we are tempted, we are inferior to the temptation.

- If we are tempted, we are more evil than other people.

- God brings temptation to us. (No, He doesn't bring it, but He allows it. See James 1:13-15.)

- Temptation doesn't accomplish anything in our lives. It's a waste of time. (No, let's give thanks for it. It has a great purpose.)

- Someday I won't be tempted. (Hah!)

- I'm tempted because I'm more important than other people.

- Temptation only comes after a great defeat. (Actually, we are most prone to temptation after great victory.)

- It doesn't cost anything to flee or resist temptation if we are in God's will. (No, in fact, it will cost you greatly at times, as it did Joseph.)

HEAT REQUIRED

As I read through the temptation Joseph faced with Potiphar's wife, I felt a little sorry for him. After all he'd been through, why couldn't God make it a little easier on the guy? The only answer to my question is: God knows what He's doing.

My friend David Owens once invited me to spend a day with him at the Museum of Flight. Dave is a terribly busy man — he manages a significant business in our area — so I knew his time was valuable. I was terribly busy at the time too.

But I've concluded that it is too easy to get caught up in

the task stuff and the thing stuff and forget about the people stuff. If you're going to have friends, you had better value them. And whatever you value you give time to. So I said yes, I'd go, and we both headed to the museum in his station wagon on a snowy day in Seattle (which doesn't happen often).

We live in an area where Boeing, the famous airplane builder, represents most of our economy. Nearly one out of three jobs in the area is related to building airplanes. Yet I'd never taken much interest in planes. I thought, It's about time I learn something about flight.

Airplanes scare me a bit. I hate getting in a 747 that is more than a quarter filled, and I despise small planes. But here we were wandering around the Museum of Flight. They had a replica of a 1902 Wright Glider, an early design of Orville and Wilbur Wright's. We even saw some of the original worktables from the first wood planes Boeing made in the 1930s. Then there was the replica of the B-29 bomber. These were all interesting.

But the Holy Spirit really got ahold of my heart as Dave and I listened to a lecture about a reconnaissance plane called the Lockheed A-12 Blackbird. The Blackbird was the plane that succeeded the U-2, the one that Gary Powers was shot down in over Russia in 1960 (when the United States officially said it wasn't spying on the Russians). After that, the defense department decided we needed better reconnaissance planes.

The Blackbird has two large engines, and most of the rest of the plane is a fuel tank. It is designed to fly at a height of more than eighty thousand feet in excess of three times the speed of sound.

The ground crews had to be specially trained to understand the nature of the fuel in these planes. Almost the entire body of the aircraft was filled with fuel, and it leaked like a sieve. The crew would be standing in a shower of jet fuel. It was a little unnerving if they had worked with other airplane fuel.

"This fuel is designed to require a special chemical called TEB (tri-ethyl-borane) in order to ignite," our lecturer said. "You could toss a lighted match into this fuel, and it would extinguish it."

"But why do they make the tanks so that the fuel leaks out?" one of the men in the crowd asked. "Can't they build them tighter than that?"

Our guide answered with a smile, "These planes are designed to work in the heavenlies, under the intense heat produced by the friction of the atmosphere against the fast-moving plane. The temperature of the surface of the plane reaches up to one thousand degrees when it's in flight. The heat causes the titanium skin of the plane to expand up to a foot on some surfaces. The expansion closes the gaps in the fuselage and stops the leakage. If we latched those planes together too tightly, they would split apart in the air.

"If you keep these planes on the ground, they leak. But if you heat them up in the heavenlies, they work great."

I think that's the way dreamers are designed by God. We're designed to work at eighty thousand feet under a great deal of heat. Isaiah aptly described people energized by the living God as those who would "soar on wings like eagles" (Is. 40:31). Without the heat of temptation, we lack the power to face the forces of resistance to our dreams. Temptation helps us soar.

HOPE UNDER PRESSURE

I have a friend who has commissioned a study to discover why so many ministers are falling into compromising sins. "If you keep seeing dead bodies floating downstream," he says, "you ought to send a scout upstream to see what's happening."

I thought about the problem of sin in church leadership in these terms. I've watched these old movies about how the British fought wars. They would line up their soldiers in neat rows. Then the American revolutionary fighters would hide behind trees and pick them off one at a time. It seems as though Christians are also marching merrily along in rows, dropping dead one by one, without stopping to ask, What is going on?

Jamie Buckingham used to tell me he thought a minister's fall could often be related to a secret suicide desire. I think this really is often the case. I also believe the growing incidence of depression in our population at large does not escape those of us in ministry. Counselors know that depression of a biochemical form or from a long-term stressful situation will lead one to make moral compromises to escape the pain.

My friend has concluded in his preliminary studies that we pastors are doing too much counseling. Could it be we've bought into a model that God never intended pastors to have? If we operate outside of our essential temperament and calling, we will be introduced to temptations God has not equipped us to face. When we operate under somebody else's idea of what the dream for us ought to be, we can lack the resources to live out the dream.

I think we in the charismatic camp too often believe that because we are filled with the Holy Spirit we are no longer human. We're very human. And there's only so much the human body and emotions can take. We can only expend so much emotional and physical energy before we begin to break down.

What do you do if the pressure and temptations of life seem too excessive for you to handle? What if you don't see the escape hatch that has been promised to us in Scripture? "God is faithful; he will not let you be tempted beyond what you can bear. But when you are tempted, he will also provide a way out so that you can stand up under it" (1 Cor. 10:13b).

In Joseph's case, his escape hatch was to leave his coat in the hands of a seductress and flee from the scene of temptation. Can you also flee from the temptation in your life? If not, you may need to stop and ask yourself, Am I operating outside of God's call on my life? An authentic dream from God will not tempt you beyond what you are able to bear.

OUR LORD'S TEMPTATIONS

It has always caught my eye that the temptations of our Lord followed His baptism by John — the time when He was endowed with the Holy Spirit. In fact, the Bible says the Spirit drove Him immediately into the wilderness to be tempted (see Matt. 4:1-11). This shows me two things: 1) God does not cause a temptation from the inside out, but He isn't shy about allowing us to walk into an environment where the heat will crank up. 2) Those of us who are called to be in the kingdom and dream dreams — however big or small — will probably face the same sort of temptations. You may be surprised to see just how similar Jesus' temptations are to your own experience.

• *The temptation to take shortcuts*
Satan offered to give Jesus all the kingdoms of the world — with no suffering required. But Jesus knew that God's plan called for Calvary. He chose to be obedient to the process as well as the goal.

Leading a congregation that is big on volunteer ministries, I've noticed people are often too impatient to nurture and pace their calling. The temptation to take shortcuts to accomplish God's work is a surefire way to burn out early.

• *The temptation of power trips and the compulsion to control*
The devil always barters in the realm of power. We've seen in the life of Joseph that God's dreams are accomplished through a servant heart.

Satan tempted Christ to throw Himself from the highest point of the temple and to prove His divinity by recovering unharmed. It was a temptation for Jesus to turn around and grasp again that which He had left in heaven. Sure, He could have done any sort of stupendous act of power to convince the world He was the Messiah. But God's true dream for His kingdom on earth would not have been realized. His dream is driven by love, not power.

In nearly every genuine move of God, we've also had the problem of leaders resorting to human power to transform lives. It is frustrating when you try to lead a group of people who will not be obedient to God. So we often develop systems to accomplish the Holy Spirit's work. It never works. There's a high level of vulnerability that God demands from all would-be dreamers in His kingdom.

• *The temptation of pleasure*

After Jesus had fasted for forty days, He was hungry, just as you or I would have been. Satan's temptation to turn stones into bread was based on the human desire for pleasure and personal comfort.

People with high levels of energy (who seem to be the ones with the greatest ease in this dream stuff) are those most often prone to the pleasure dynamic in their lives. So the nature of the best dreamers may leave them more prone to pleasure temptation.

My pleasure of choice has become food. Even as I write this I'm about fifteen pounds overweight. In all honesty, it's because I give in to the pleasure dynamic. Rather than stopping to exercise and rest properly, it's more fun just to eat a meal. It satisfies a weary body.

OK. I've confessed my sin. Now why don't you think about your own? Your pleasure temptation may seem as innocent as my overeating or as obvious as abusing drugs or alcohol.

The trap of sexual sin has received a lot of attention recently. One counselor thinks we, as church people, talk too easily about sexual sin. She believes that discussing these kinds of sin openly actually causes them to happen more. I agree with her.

It's apparent that temptation takes a legitimate gift from God and pushes it to the point of harm. Sin is often taking a good thing and overdoing it. Who would argue that it's better to have enough food to live in health and strength before the Lord than to be starving? And who would be so foolish as to say that God thought sex was dirty? But, nonetheless, the pleasure dynamic is a real obstacle to a life-style of power.

- *Almost is close enough.*

Many churches in the United States are not growing but instead are experiencing a decline in attendance. I think one of the major reasons is that we Christians have grown accustomed to being happy with "almost being close enough."

In Christ's temptation it was clear that He wasn't willing to settle for "almost being close enough." He vigorously refuted the devil with every temptation. Joseph had the same commitment to excellence. He would not allow himself to be anything less than an excellent servant (Gen. 39). Simple obedience wasn't enough for him. He had to be a servant who made his master rich.

I am persuaded that the reason more people aren't filling our churches is that "almost" is good enough for us. Dreaming demands a cry for excellence in our lives — excellence in integrity, character and performance.

OTHER TRAPS DREAMERS FACE

When we are under pressure, we are also faced with powerful temptations to attitudes that will eventually choke out our dreams.

- The spirit of victimization.

  This is most noticeable when you feel like you're being picked on, or you are suffering temptation you feel others have never known. As Joseph languished in prison, he refused to give way to victimized thinking — though he was certainly a victim.

  We are all victims. We are victims of the fall in the garden. We are victims of our own parents' dysfunctions. But when we're victimized, we have a greater capacity for compassion.

- This won't happen to me again.

  I've often said, "I'll never let this happen to me again." The fact is that it often happens again anyway. That kind of defensive living works against offensive living for your dream.

- I'll get even with them.

  Retaliation is a distraction and a real drain on dreams.

- I'm fine. It didn't bother me a bit.

  This kind of denial only sets us up for time bombs to go off later in our lives. I've seen friends explode over pain they had felt ten years earlier, and then they saw their dreams evaporate overnight.

  Good, wholesome, assertive confrontation is good. Follow Jesus' instructions on confronting a believer who sins against you (Matt. 18:15-20).

- Cynicism.

  Living around Christians can cause cynicism — I'll admit that. But the author of Hebrews warned us that roots of bitterness can cause trouble and defile many (Heb. 12:15). Cynics often get indignant over shortcomings they see in the church. I don't think God is surprised with our temptations or sins. So why should we be?

Cynicism, especially a jaundiced attitude toward all who would claim God's name, only destroys the dreams that could fill our hearts.

THE BIG TEMPTATION

Over the years I've made statements from time to time about being called to build the kingdom. Now I see this notion may be a dreamer's greatest temptation.

I recently read a penetrating comment in a book titled *The Gift of Time*. "Jesus urged people to enter the kingdom, not to build it."[1] The Holy Spirit now causes my heart to wince when I or others say, "We are building the kingdom." None of us is called to build the kingdom. In all Christ's statements about the kingdom, we are called to enter into it. The expression of our dreams is not the building of the kingdom but rather the manifestation and expression of His kingdom already being here.

So if you're a dreamer, don't get too heady. If the kingdom isn't already built into your heart, you'll never give a clear expression of it. If His kingdom is already here, we're only giving expression to what belongs to the King.

This truth also puts us in a humbling place when the building program doesn't work or the new TV satellite doesn't get purchased or the Christian education wing doesn't get built. The kingdom is still there whether these things happen or not.

When it comes to the kingdom we Americans particularly have a fixation with the visible. We are the consummate innovators and endless builders. Now there's nothing wrong with this. But rather than saying we're building God's kingdom by building a Christian education wing, we ought simply to say we're building a Christian education wing. God alone knows what will happen.

But the kingdom is here on earth, and it is hoped that it will manifest itself in that building over there while the kids study.

I'm frightened of kingdom builders. I think God's dreams have a lot less to do with stuff and a lot more to do with heart.

JOSEPH'S SECRET POWER IN FACING THE DREAM SEDUCERS

Earlier in this book I referred to Joseph as a template. Let's place that template over our lives again and see whether we have at least three of the traits that can be recognized in Joseph's life as he resisted temptation.

- He knew who his real audience was.

  In his book *The Becomer*, J. Keith Miller has a wonderful description of what it means to have Jesus as your Lord. He says having Jesus as your Lord means having Him as your audience of significance. What's an audience of significance? you ask. It is the person whose face you see in the crowd.

  I played Little League baseball. I would often glance into the stands and look for family members. My grandmother was usually there. Her face would stand out in the crowd to me. She made me feel like Dave Winfield in the World Series.

  We're to see Jesus' face in the crowd.

  How did Joseph and our Lord face temptation? They saw God as their audience of significance. They were living their lives to hear the living God say, "Well done, thou good and faithful servant." This gives a power that cannot be beaten by temptation.

- He knew who he was.

Self-identity is essential in facing temptation. Joseph wouldn't behave in a manner that
was below his awareness of his identity. He
knew he was chosen for high purposes so he
behaved with high instincts.

Who are you in Christ? Before starting on
what we are going to do for God, we need to
establish who we are in God. Our behavior will
correspond with the way we see ourselves. In
Scripture, identity always precedes behavior
(see the call to holy behavior in Rom. 12:1-2 in
light of our position "in Christ" in Eph. 2:6-7).

Remember in chapter 7 when we said God is
more interested in who we become than in
what we do? People who want to do something
to prove who they are frighten me. As we become sons and daughters of God first, then our
behavior as dreamers will follow perfectly in
His plan.

This was one of the secrets to Joseph's
power. He knew who he was, and he knew how
someone like him behaved.

- He possessed sincerity of heart.

The movie *Leap of Faith* came out in December 1992. I went to see this movie with my
brother and my dad on Christmas Day. We sat
in the front row. It was a great show — I have
to admit I only slept through a couple of
scenes.

Some people may be appalled that I would
go to see such a movie because it was mocking
a traveling evangelist. That's why I took my
dad. He can verify that I wasn't misbehaving.
The movie was actually about a traveling
evangelist who was *not* a Christian. He and his
team had only one aim: to bilk a small town
out of enough money to move on to the next big

city.

It was actually a parody of the life of a false evangelist caught by the media a couple of years ago. The real false evangelist had concealed an earphone in his ear by which he was given information about people in the crowd. He would then share the information as though he had received words of knowledge. (By words of knowledge we mean special insight and knowledge about someone's life.)

Steve Martin played the leading role effectively, dancing and prancing like a true sawdust evangelist. Through most of the movie I sensed we were in for a surprise. It came, as I had expected, at the end.

A fake healing had been set up for almost every night of the crusade, but in the last big scene of the movie, a young boy was actually healed. Jonas Nightingale, the evangelist, was confronted with the sincerity of a healed child. This child believed the words that the evangelist had spoken, acted on them and was healed. The human heart has been able to handle the scandals of the last few years because true sincerity and true integrity always win out. For me, that was the message of the film.

The film gives us some insight into our culture. People are not as turned off to our message as we may think. It's our methods that perplex them. The false prophets that have come into our midst are disconcerting. But there is always a place for true sincerity. By sincerity we mean "to will one thing" (as Kierkegaard would say). Joseph had purity of heart. He had simplicity. Life wasn't complex for him. When temptation and iniquity confront sincerity, they collapse as crippled before the power of God.

LIFE APPLICATION

- Can you discuss your greatest temptation with a confidant? Have you ever?

- Have you ever noticed a time in your life when temptation has frightened you and made you stop dreaming?

- Do you ever thank God for the temptation in your life? Have you developed a practice of confession of sin in an appropriate manner?

- Can you detect any area of your life where you may be impacted by cynicism?

If your dreams have been interrupted by dream seducers, I encourage you to find a trusted friend or pastor and work through the preceding questions with him or her. There is no reason to miss out on soaring like an eagle.

If you're going through a time of temptation, don't be discouraged. Consider this insight from author Hannah Whitall Smith.

> The Christian life is to be throughout a warfare, and that especially when seated in heavenly places in Christ Jesus. We are to wrestle against spiritual enemies there, whose power and skill to tempt us must doubtless be far superior to any we have heretofore encountered. As a fact, temptations generally increase in strength tenfold after we have entered into the interior life, rather than decrease. And no amount or sort of them must ever for a moment lead us to suppose that we have not really found the true abiding place. Strong temptations are generally a sign of great grace, rather than of little grace.[2]

TWELVE

STEWARDING DREAMS

The plan seemed good to Pharaoh and to all his officials. So Pharaoh asked them, "Can we find anyone like this man, one in whom is the spirit of God?"

Then Pharaoh said to Joseph, "Since God has made all this known to you, there is no one so discerning and wise as you. You shall be in charge of my palace, and all my people are to submit to your orders. Only with respect to the throne will I be greater than you."

Joseph was thirty years old when he entered the service of Pharaoh king of Egypt. And Joseph went out from Pharaoh's presence and traveled throughout Egypt. During the seven years of abundance the land produced plentifully. Joseph collected all the food produced in those seven years of abundance in Egypt and stored it in the cities. In each city he put the food grown in the fields surrounding it.

The seven years of abundance in Egypt came to an end, and the seven years of famine began, just as Joseph had said.

And all the countries came to Egypt to buy grain from Joseph, because the famine was severe in all the world (Gen. 41:37-40,46-48,53,57).

SCENE: *Pharaoh's private treasury, 1690 B.C.*

PHARAOH: O gods, I know that I can trust this man. He knew what those blasted cows meant in my dream — the seven large, fat ones followed by the seven starving, skinny ones. They haunted me night after night.

Fortunately, my lazy cupbearer remembered this young Hebrew prisoner.

I can see that he is trustworthy in his heart. The warden informed me that he had managed the affairs of the prison well. Such a one ought to be bitter, but I see no anger in his eyes, only gratitude for an opportunity to serve.

Potiphar even pulled me aside and let me know that the man was actually innocent. I understood why Potiphar had to accuse him. I would have done the same. And yet this Hebrew Joseph stands like an oak. I know what I will do. I will make him steward of my entire empire. I will give him an Egyptian name — Zaphenath-Paneah. I will give him the daughter of the priest of Asenath for his wife.

There is something of the gods upon and within this one. He is trustworthy, so trust I will give him. O gods, may I not be wrong.

It was a big break for Joseph — from the prison cell to the Pharaoh's palace. I can see the headlines now: "Hebrew boy gets top government post." "Ex-con to lead country." Many people probably thought he was the luckiest guy in the world. All he did was interpret a couple of dreams and bam! — he gets instant power.

But Joseph knew that every bit of responsibility that Pharaoh gave him had been earned over many years of faithful stewardship. First it was for Potiphar, then for the warden of the jail. Potiphar trusted Joseph so much that the only thing he concerned himself about was what he was going to eat. The jail warden was also satisfied — he paid no attention to anything under Joseph's care. Pharaoh was in for a very pleasant surprise when he chose Joseph as steward.

A steward is "one who acts as a supervisor or administrator, as of finances and property, for another or others" (according to Webster's dictionary).

Stewards live with striking realities.

- What they control is not their own.

- They will give an account for how they have handled another's affairs.

- They may not reap any reward from the profits made.

No, stewards are not commission salesmen or investment brokers. They are people who give their lives handling the affairs of another without the certainty of any reward.

As Christians, we are called to be stewards. Paul referred to Christian leaders of his day as "stewards of the mysteries of God" (1 Cor. 4:1, KJV). I think the same holds true for us.

I have picked up a few observations about stewardship over the years. One thing I hear over and over is:

- Start where you are.

When I started writing and leading a church, Jamie Buckingham told me:

- Anything worth doing is worth doing properly.

Finally, one of my old college professors shared with me:

- Be faithful with the brains you have, and they might grow. You never know.

BIBLICAL STEWARDSHIP

Again, it will be like a man going on a journey, who called his servants and entrusted his property to them. To one he gave five talents of money, to another two talents, and to another one talent, each according to his ability. Then he went on his journey. The man who had received the five talents went at once and put his money to work and gained five more. So also, the one with the two talents gained two more. But the man who had received the one talent went off, dug a hole in the ground and hid his master's money.

After a long time the master of those servants returned and settled accounts with them. The man who had received the five talents brought the other five. "Master," he said, "you entrusted me with five talents. See, I have gained five more."

His master replied, "Well done, good and faithful servant! You have been faithful with a few things; I will put you in charge of many things. Come and share your master's happiness!"

The man with the two talents also came. "Master," he said, "you entrusted me with two talents; see, I have gained two more."

His master replied, "Well done, good and faithful servant! You have been faithful with a few things; I will put you in charge of many things. Come and share your master's happiness!"

Then the man who had received the one talent came. "Master," he said, "I knew that you are a hard man, harvesting where you have not sown and gathering where you have not scattered seed. So I was afraid and went out and hid your talent in the ground. See, here is what belongs to you."

His master replied, "You wicked, lazy servant! So you knew that I harvest where I have not sown and gather where I have not scattered seed? Well then, you should have put my money on deposit with the bankers, so that when I returned I would have received it back with interest.

"Take the talent from him and give it to the one who has the ten talents. For everyone who has will be given more, and he will have an abundance. Whoever does not have, even what he has will be taken from him. And throw that worthless servant outside, into the darkness, where there will be weeping and gnashing of teeth" (Matt. 25:14-28)

This is a fascinating parable. It shows several axioms

about stewarding that are worth noting.

- We aren't all equally gifted. We appreciate skill so highly in our culture that we become overly impressed with someone who is highly gifted. Actually, this will only cause us to trip up if we are not careful.

- We are all to be equally accountable. The issue is not how gifted we are, but how we handle the giftedness that has been handed to us.

- We are all equally important. It is interesting to me that the owner became so angry with the one who had the least number of talents. It is because each gift handed out is equally important. Whether you have much or little talent, start where you are and work with what you have.

VITAL AREAS OF STEWARDSHIP

We are called to steward several vital areas of our Christian lives, and we can't afford to overlook any of them. How we handle these areas can make the difference between a dream completed and a dream left unfulfilled.

Let's outline these vital areas of stewardship.

Money

Money is becoming more and more an irrational concept. One of my acquaintances believes this is because we have detached it from a gold standard. I am not an economist, but who knows? It may be true.

I do know that money was a very serious business to Jesus. He talked about it more than any other topic. In another parable about stewarding, Jesus made the following statement:

Whoever can be trusted with very little can also be trusted with much, and whoever is dishonest with very little will also be dishonest with much. So if you have not been trustworthy in handling worldly wealth, who will trust you with true riches? And if you have not been trustworthy with someone else's property, who will give you property of your own?" (Luke 16:10-12).

Our money is the most visible expression of the way we steward the life that God has given us.

I have seen many dreams stand incomplete due to misuse of money. The misuse can range from the excessive use of credit to the excessive pursuit of wealth. God's dreams flourish when one is liberal with giving money. But it goes further than that. In the words of the great historical church leader John Wesley, "Christians ought to react to money in the following ways: earn all the money they can, give all the money they can, and then save all the money they can."

How you handle your money will determine the extent to which your dreams will grow. I have had to learn this in leading a large church. I was never trained to manage, but now I manage what in today's terms is a mid-size business. I am learning that businesspeople who learn to manage money well have gained great and deep spiritual insights in their lives by dealing with this entity Christ called a god — mammon.

Count on it! The way you steward the money you have will determine the quality of dreaming you will experience. Jesus said it was so. How you handle your money determines how He will entrust you with new visions and dreams.

Do you tithe? Do you set aside money for the poor? Do you save?

So many Christians react to money only on an emotional level. Paul talks about money as being very indicative of our true *spiritual* state.

> Out of the most severe trial, their overflowing joy and their extreme poverty welled up in rich generosity....They [the Macedonians] gave as much as they were able and even beyond their ability....They gave themselves first to the Lord and then to us in keeping with God's will (2 Cor. 8:2-3,5; see also 1 Cor. 16:1-2).

Money needs to be stewarded as though it belongs to the Lord. It ought to be handled very strategically as we steward our lives.

Dreamers of God need to spend much more time studying money and how it works. I would challenge you to do this as we move toward the end of this century when many are predicting challenging economic times.

Time

The psalmist cried out to God in Psalm 90:12: "Teach us to number our days aright, that we may gain a heart of wisdom."

The development of a strong spiritual life and sensitivity to dreaming takes time. The great devotional writer Evelyn Underhill says:

> Plainly then, it is essential to give time or to get time somehow for self training in this love and this prayer, in order to develop those (spiritual powers). It is true that in their essence they are given, but the gift is only fully made our own by a patient and generous effort of the soul. Spiritual achievement costs much, though never as much as it is worth.[1]

What Evelyn Underhill was saying is that we cannot measure the time we put into our spiritual lives on the basis of returns. We walk by faith and not by sight (2 Cor. 5:7). When we invest time in the spiritual development of our dreams, it may not look as if the payoffs are there. But they are.

While in the middle of writing this chapter, I received a phone call from a friend of mine whose own ministry is extremely businesslike, especially in the way he handles time.

We exchanged pleasantries about the well-being of one another's families. We both care deeply about one another. But our conversation began to flow from item to item, scheduling, events, the new year ahead and some discussion about what we anticipated the Lord might be doing in our lives.

At the end of the conversation my friend made a comment that caught my ear. He said, "This was a great conversation, extremely productive, the kind I like to have."

I began laughing. He didn't take the time to ask why I was laughing. But his comment sounded so strange to me. It made me feel like an item on a corporate agenda. I know my friend well, and I know it was just a manifestation of his personality and the world he lives in. But it made me wonder whether Jesus would own a daily planner. I'm not so sure He would. Just read John 11.

Planning and strategic thinking are important, however. After Joseph had interpreted Pharaoh's dream — that seven years of plenty would be followed by seven years of famine — he didn't just sit back and wait for it to happen. He made plans to store food during the prosperous years so that the people could survive the years of destitution.

The stewarding of time involves planning and identifying priorities, goals and aims. I have to walk through these things with our staff here at the church periodically, and I also like to operate from a plan for the year at home.

However, I've become acutely aware that this may not be what the Bible has in mind about teaching us to mark our time (Ps. 39:4). Is it true that time equals money? People do behave that way these days. In fact, we've discovered in leading our church that it's easier to ask someone for a hundred dollars than it is for an hour of his or her time. Time is a precious commodity in our culture.

Stewarding time from a biblical standpoint means doing the right thing at the right time more than doing as much as possible in the shortest possible time.

Parents know that the synonym for love is time. So do couples who have learned to nurture their love over the years. Time is love. And time is a calling. Why don't you try to put that kind of thinking in your mind next time you sit and contemplate your plan for the coming year?

As I'm writing, we're coming to the end of a year. Next year I am going to try exactly what I'm advising you to do. I'm going to view my time as love and my time as calling. (In other words, I will give my time to what I love and what I'm called to.)

I've come to believe that *busy* and *Christian* are antithetical terms. Christ is to come alive in the events of every moment for us. Where we spend our time is where our love is.

I am certain when some of you started reading this section about time, you broke out into a cold sweat. Fears of being confronted with your own procrastination filled your heart and mind. And you immediately reached for your daily planner.

Could it be that stewarding our time could mean deliberately wasting some of it? To remain healthy every human being needs strategic and deliberate time-wasting. We need activities during which we can take off our watches and just watch the sun. We need activities that don't have any goal or point to them.

To sum it up, the dreamer stewards time not only as a vehicle for accomplishment, but he stewards time as love and especially time as calling. I think this is what Christ had in mind in Acts 1 when the disciples asked him, "Is now the time for the kingdom?" He said it wasn't the time yet. Those things were left in the hands of the Father. God has set times for accomplishments in each of our lives. Our strategic thinking won't speed them up, but our deliberate and strategic devotion to Him in our time will make certain we are never late for anything He has in mind for us.

Energies

Dreamers learn to steward their energies as well. I ran track in school. I preferred short sprints over long distances. My race was the fifty-yard dash. However, I was asked on several occasions to try long-distance relay runs. It's very difficult to get the swing of that kind of running when you're used to being a sprinter. I could rarely compete with the strategic way the long-distance runners had learned to pace their energies.

As Christians we are all called to be long-distance runners. How strong we are at the end of the race is more important to the Lord than how quickly we move to the front at the beginning.

As dreamers we'll need to steward our emotional, spiritual and intellectual energies to accomplish God's task. Being unwise about the expenditure of any of these energies in our lives can undermine the culmination of all our dreams.

Memories

Dreamers steward their memories as sources of courage. This is often an overlooked reality by Western Christians, but if you read the Bible closely, you'll find that remembering is an important task of the believer.

Remember the Sabbath (Ex. 20:8).

KEEPING YOUR DREAMS ALIVE

> Each of you is to take up a stone on his shoulder,
> according to the number of the tribes of the Isra-
> elites, to serve as a sign among you. In the fu-
> ture, when your children ask you, "What do
> these stones mean?" tell them that the flow of
> the Jordan was cut off before the ark of the cove-
> nant of the Lord. When it crossed the Jordan, the
> waters of the Jordan were cut off. *These stones
> are to be a memorial to the people of Israel forever*
> (Josh. 4:5b-7, italics added).

> "This is my body, which is for you; do this in
> remembrance of me." In the same way, after sup-
> per he took the cup, saying, "This cup is the new
> covenant in my blood; do this, whenever you
> drink it, in remembrance of me" (1 Cor. 11:24b-
> 25; see also Matt. 26:27-29; Mark 14:25; Luke
> 22:17-18,30).

Do you steward your memories? Do you realize this is
one of the main reasons for our worship times and taking
communion? Sunday, the first day of the week, is a day to
remember the resurrection.

Stewards of dreams have the regular discipline of celebrating memorials. I've begun keeping a journal to help
me do this. I keep records of significant things the Lord
has either done or spoken in my life. I find great solace
when I go back and read recollections of God's working in
my past. I also read the history of some of the great
events in Scripture. The spirit of remembrance fills my
heart, which empowers me for the present and the future.

Our Words

Scripture has many valuable insights into what we say.
Here's just a sample found in Proverbs 16:23.

> A wise man's heart guides his mouth.

From the fruit of his mouth a man's stomach is filled; with the harvest from his lips he is satisfied (Prov. 18:20).

The tongue has the power of life and death, and those who love it eat its fruit (Prov. 18:21).

For out of the overflow of the heart the mouth speaks (Matt. 12:34b).

But I tell you that men will have to give account on the day of judgment for every careless word they have spoken. For by your words you will be acquitted, and by your words you will be condemned (Matt. 12:36-37).

The stewarding of our speech builds our faith to prepare us to be part of God's dreams. I'm not speaking here of some of the more extreme "name it and claim it" practices. I'm speaking of the biblical principle that what you say to yourself will shape you. The words you speak about your future help set the course of your life. And what you say about others will shape them as well. So let your words be filled with faith and grace.

Our speech about God's dreams in our lives is one of the most important and delicate aspects of our walk in Christ. We can't underestimate Christ's warning that we will give an account as to how we've stewarded words (Matt. 12:36). I think the reason for this is that God created words for distinct purposes. Words are the vehicles by which we identify most closely with God the Creator. I believe our ability to speak is what brings us most closely to being in the image of God. After all, by speaking He created.

Spiritual Gifts

We have different gifts, *according to the grace given us*. If a man's gift is prophesying, let him use it in proportion to his faith. If it is serving, let him serve; if it is teaching, let him teach; if it is encouraging, let him encourage; if it is contributing to the needs of others, let him give generously; if it is leadership, let him govern diligently; if it is showing mercy, let him do it cheerfully (Rom. 12:6-8, italics added).

Each of us has been endowed with spiritual grace by the Holy Spirit. By the contribution of all these gifts God's dream for this planet is fulfilled (Eph. 4:11-13).

In our congregation we have developed a terrific course we call Church 201. A member of our pastoral leadership team, John Decker, has developed this course to help individuals assess not only their personality temperaments but also their spiritual giftings and inclinations.

One of the vital parts of this course is the teaching on the call to steward these gifts of the Spirit. No one owns the Spirit's gifts. The Holy Spirit has dispersed these gifts on every member according to His purposes (1 Cor. 12:11).

If I pray in the Spirit, I am to steward that gift to the highest possible pleasure of God. If my gift is prophecy, I am to do it in a manner that will glorify Him most highly. These gifts do not belong to me. They belong to Him. Like my money, time, energies, memories and words, I am to steward them as though they belonged to God.

Relationships

Therefore, as God's chosen people, holy and dearly loved, clothe yourselves with compassion, kindness, humility, gentleness and patience.

> Bear with each other and forgive whatever griev-
> ances you may have against one another. Forgive
> as the Lord forgave you. And over all these vir-
> tues put on love, which binds them all together
> in perfect unity (Col. 3:12-14).

I enjoyed meditating on this theme for several hours the other day in preparation for writing this text. What a powerful teaching on how we should steward relation-ships! One of the first relationships I thought of is my relationship with my children. My children do not belong to me, but they have been handed to me temporarily by God. Whenever I officiate in the dedication of children, I remind parents of this. Our children belong to God, but we are to steward them.

I also have come to believe that valued friends in my life can never be replaced. When my friend Jamie Buck-ingham died last year, I had no idea of the impact it would have on my life. Our biweekly phone calls came to an end. A trusted friend, who helped me work through many a difficulty on a manuscript or an issue in our church, was gone. He will never be replaced.

In our highly mobile society we suffer a great deal from the mis-stewardship of relationships and friendships in our lives. Christians hop and move about from church to church, bifurcating relationships and wondering why they are prone to feelings of isolation. I think that the perpetual immaturity of many Christians in the United States is due to the devaluation of *koinonia* or social part-nership in our lives.

Relationships ought not to be a point of bondage, but they certainly are to be a point of responsibility and stew-ardship. In the last year I have come to value my friends more than ever. I think the loss of Jamie has helped me do that. I have also greatly weakened my relationship with three or four good friends because I didn't keep suf-ficient contact with them. I foolishly believed that there were many other friends to move on to.

Friendships that God brings into our lives are His gifts to us. They belong to Him. We are to nurture them, steward them, feed them and invest in them.

When storms come into our lives, we need friends to rely upon. Without nurturing these relationships, they are rarely there when we need them. True biblical dreamers know how to network their lives and trust the gifts of friendship that God gives.

Christians are not necessarily limited to Christian friends, either. I have found great friendship in an unchurched, Jewish attorney. We meet two, three or four times a year, but he has counseled and guided me through many issues with his expertise and friendship. There is a relationship there that goes way beyond a client and attorney relationship. I believe that it comes from the dynamic of the Holy Spirit. I choose to steward this relationship.

The church I pastor has grown by several thousands of people. As a result, I have found myself encouraging people to get involved in small groups, investing in five to six friends as a means of spiritual growth.

We need a revolution in the church of the United States — a revolution that will work against the mobility into which our economic enterprise has forced us. We need a revolution that will cause us to value relationships as gifts from God.

Commitments

Then Jacob made a vow (Gen. 28:20).

Fulfill your vows to the Most High (Ps. 50:14).

I am under vows to you, O God (Ps. 56:12).

If you are like me, you have trouble saying no. It is

difficult for me to be asked to speak somewhere and have to say no. I think part of the reason is that I am afraid I will miss out on something. But mostly I can't bear disappointing the other person.

I am not really a people-pleaser — I don't particularly care what others think of me. I just have great distress when leaving someone in need of help. A friend of mine tells me, "Doug, you're a great codependent."

Those who see the fulfillment of God's working in their lives take their commitments very seriously. People always say that a man is no better than his word. I would add that a man or woman is no stronger in Christ than his or her efforts to keep commitments that he or she has made to Christ and others.

My effort to discipline my commitments is causing me to make fewer and fewer commitments all the time. Schedules look entirely different on pieces of paper than they feel like when they are lived out. Be careful of the number of commitments you make. Steward how many you make, and keep the ones you do.

God works strongly on behalf of the people who keep their word once they have committed. Holy Spirit, help us to do that daily!

TRUE AND FALSE STEWARDSHIP

Today we have an essential call to be stewards. As we relate to our call, all of us are tempted to fall into pseudo-patterns of stewardship. Two of these patterns are prevalent in the church in the United States: consumerism and spectatorship.

Stewards vs. Consumers

Stewards view the resources that have been extended to them as a reason for accountability as to how they live. Consumers, on the other hand, try to get in on the latest religious experience. Consumers are purchasers of religious information, experiences and events. This is vastly different from being a steward.

What if the high school program at your church is a bummer? A steward would look for ways to improve it. A consumer would find a church with a better program.

Stewards vs. Spectators

Frankly, I think the charismatic movement has lent itself far too much to the theatrics of the front platform. We have created spectators, and all of us have tended to let the ultra-gifted take over too much responsibility.

Spectators want to watch other people do their thing. Spectators have been taught and trained to be thrilled with the latest event or spiritual fad.

Stewards meet together instead to learn new patterns of behaving like disciples, to hear the Scriptures proclaimed in public worship and praise, and to bring their hearts open and ready to the Lord's leading.

We church leaders live with the reality that 15 percent of the people carry 85 percent of the financial load in most churches today. Membership costs too little in most churches across the country. I suspect this is one reason church attendance has fallen off. None of us wants to be part of something that costs little.

We can't be casual members of the body of Christ. We are stewards of His work in one another. We are to be joined together relationally, not just on the rosters and roles of churches.

Growing churches and growing Christians at the end of this millennium will hand in their religious consumer credit cards and season passes to the latest show. They will gladly be left off membership roles if they can be participants and stewards vitally at work doing the serious work of the kingdom. In this we'll see not only our dreams fulfilled, but God's great dream of the fulfillment of His kingdom.

LIFE APPLICATION

There are several traits you can find in someone who is stewarding his or her gifts. Why don't you muse over this list and consider your own life. If you lay the template of Joseph's life over your stewarding, how will you come out?

- Stewards take the long view.

- Stewards are trustworthy.

- Stewards see opportunities in hidden places.

- Stewards bring people and events together.

- Stewards are resilient under pressure.

- Stewards cheer on other dreamers.

- Stewards view every moment of their lives as an investment.

- Stewards are committed to leaving a legacy behind them.

Now ask yourself these specific questions.

- Do you tithe and give 10 percent of your income to your local congregation? (Mal. 3:10).

- Would Pharaoh trust you with his money if he saw your checkbook?

- Do you recognize the danger of being a consumer vs. a steward? Can you identify at least three areas in your life where you may be consuming rather than stewarding?

- Do you steward the planet? Do you recycle, and are you careful about the use of the resources we have on this planet? This is one of the great areas of witness open to us at the end of the twentieth century.

- Have you said no to excessive opportunities lately?

- Are you celebrating memories of God's work in your life?

If you are frustrated with the lack of fulfilled dreaming in your life, could it be that the stewardship element has been left wanting? Year by year, Joseph kept his nose to the grind, investing in small steps of obedience every day. He could be counted on in the mundane, small stuff. Can you? Can I?

I would like to introduce you to two people in our congregation who model powerful stewardship.

The first is Janice. Janice was a gifted Bible teacher. She died last year after a six-month battle with terminal brain cancer. Janice was one of the most impressive Christians I have ever met. She was highly intelligent and very gifted spiritually. She and her husband gave their lives to multiple charitable and kingdom-oriented ministries in our community.

Knowing she had teaching skills, she went into a golf club one day and invited people to a Bible study in her home. Many in the club were Jewish, and most of the other members were non-Christians, though some of them did attend church. To her surprise, a dozen or so turned up at her house for a Bible study. The study grew and grew until there were dozens of people attending. Many of them were individuals who would have been considered up-and-outers, who never had the opportunity to listen to the gospel before.

Janice also had a burden for the people who lived in her neighborhood. So she started a Bible study group for women. It grew to have multiple teachers and numbered as many as three hundred in attendance. She stewarded her gifts faithfully, and God produced the fruit. She saw a need and reached out to meet it. It is no wonder that her life was expressed in having great joy.

I was privileged to be the officiating pastor at her funeral service. Nearly twelve hundred people attended. Individual after individual shared how her life had impacted and shaped them. Her ability to steward her gifts had impacted more people than she would ever have imagined.

Janice was a dreamer who left a great impact. One thing I have noted about great dreamers is that they leave a great void when they're gone. The other day my wife commented about one of our friends who passed on to be with the Lord. "There is a great presence missing," she said.

When I see this happen, my prayer is, "Lord, fill that void with another dreamer."

In our congregation we have what we call cluster groups. These are teams of five to ten people who take on either a mission or benevolent ministry in our community. One cluster group is led by a businessman named Tim. Tim runs his own construction company, and he specializes in remodeling. Not only does he run his business to support his family, but he says, "I do it so I can finance my real ministry."

During the past several years, Tim and his team of contractors, at their own expense, have built eight churches in Papua, New Guinea, and Guatemala. Last summer they built a church on an Indian reservation in the state of Washington.

Tim and the team all bought T-shirts with large letters on it — IMPACT! They wear them around our church often. They want others to see that God has given them a dream to impact the world through building churches where they could not otherwise be built. They don't wait for someone else to buy the material. They believe God will provide it. They are very submitted to the leadership of our church. Of course, we pray for them and lend assistance as a congregation as they share their gifts.

Tim knows that the kingdom has come. He is not building it, but he is giving expression of the kingdom that is in his heart. His dreams excite me and multitudes of others. I listen when he and his team members talk about what they are going to do this summer.

I mention Tim because he sees himself as a steward of the gifts and resources that God has given him in this life. He has managed these resources and aligned them with the dream that God has given him. And he is filled with joy, as few people experience these days.

Tim and Janice are not religious professionals or board members. They do not have pulpits. You wouldn't pick them out for their extraordinary talents.

Yet they have influenced people in ways that I never could as a pastor. God needs dreamers more than spectators. He cries out for the church to be freed of consumerism and to return to stewardship.

THIRTEEN

TRANSITIONAL PEOPLE

When Joseph's brothers saw that their father was dead, they said, "What if Joseph holds a grudge against us and pays us back for all the wrongs we did to him?" So they sent word to Joseph, saying, "Your father left these instructions before he died: 'This is what you are to say to Joseph: I ask you to forgive your brothers the sins and the wrongs they committed in treating you so badly.' Now please forgive the sins of the servants of the God of your father." When their message came to him, Joseph wept.

His brothers then came and threw themselves down before him. "We are your slaves," they said.

But Joseph said to them, "Don't be afraid. Am I in the place of God? You intended to harm me, but God intended it for good to accomplish what is now being done, the saving of many lives. So then, don't be afraid. I will provide for you and your children." And he reassured them and spoke kindly to them (Gen. 50:15-21).

SCENE: *Joseph's receiving room, 1659 B.C.*

JOSEPH: I can see the fear in their eyes. Now that my father, Jacob, is gone, my brothers, who have competed with me, undermined me and hated me, are totally dependent on me. I could punish them. I could even put them to death. But, no, this would only continue what has cursed our family for generations.

How can I but love and forgive them, after all that You, my God, have done for me? The hatred must end here. We must truly connect as the chosen people that You will use to build a great nation. Someone must show a greatness and stand against that which would destroy us and make us a small people.

Now I see Your dream. You wish us to be a great people. But this will require a people with great hearts. We must set the stage for what you have in mind. I will acknowledge my emotions and make a choice to be a bridge to healing.

WHAT IS A TRANSITIONAL PERSON?

One author recently wrote a book titled *I'm Dysfunctional, You're Dysfunctional.* The author challenges the twelve-step movement and suggests that our fixation with dysfunctionality has opened wide the door to evading personal responsibility.[1] To some extent her thoughts may be a warning that requires some consideration.

However, no one who has his or her eyes open can doubt the impact of alcoholism, drug addiction, machismo and depression as they have been perpetuated through generation after generation of our families.

Depression is rising by the decade in our century. It is caused in great part by the fact that people who are genetically predisposed to depression often have larger families. The breakdown of family structures and the stress-filled pace of our life-styles are also contributing to the increase of depression. The impact of alcoholism has also proven to be multigenerational.

In the study of dysfunctions and their effect on homes, recovery workers have developed the term *transitional persons*. Transitional persons are those who stand up and stop addictive and destructive patterns in their families. I have seen them in my church. These are brave figures who say, "This is it. I will not be an addict like the others in my family."

Professionals have found that these transitional people not only introduce an end to the dysfunction in their own lives, but they also set in motion healing that moves both ways generationally.

Often these dysfunctions are called impulse control disorders. Every Tuesday night in our own congregation we have multiple twelve-step groups. Our aim is to make a place for brave transitional people like our template Joseph.

In their book titled *Living on the Border of Disorder*, Dan and Cherry Boone O'Neill have listed several of these impulse control disorders with which millions of families are struggling. They include in their list:

- Alcoholism
- Drug abuse

- Bulimia

- Anorexia

- Overeating

- Sexual addiction

- Manic-depression

- Pornography addiction

- Compulsive gambling

- Compulsive stealing or lying[2]

FAMILY DYSFUNCTIONS THAT STOP DREAMING

As I've said earlier, I think God had a hidden agenda in removing Joseph from his family of origin. Competitiveness was rampant, and deception was obsessive. One brother entered into a sexual relationship with his father's concubine. The patterns of sickness were deep and strong.

It could be that many of our dreams are left unfulfilled because we haven't taken seriously the impact of our families of origin on our lives. One hundred percent of us are impacted by our families of origin. But, of course, there are degrees of impact. Some may only be negatively impacted in 5 percent of their lives. Others are immobilized and are unable to function normally in life because of the fear and addictive patterns that have filled their homes of origin.

Joseph represents for us those bold individuals who say no to dysfunction. They are transitional people who set the stage for entire families to break through into health. The type of life-style we have developed in America is filled with ill health. The loss of the extended family and the abuse of authority are causes as well as symptoms of a breakdown of our basic family unit.

As a pastor I have noted that one can predict the ease

of success for a marriage, a career or a continued relationship with the Lord by asking a few questions about the individual's family. I have warned many a would-be husband that a wife's attitude toward her father or mother would soon be her reaction to him. I have also warned many women to watch how their would-be husbands treated their mothers and how they submitted to their fathers' authority. I can predict that the wife would be treated with the same respect or lack thereof.

Joseph shows us that there is hope. He also enlightens us to see that these issues must be faced. The naming of his son Manasseh, meaning "I have forgotten my family," suggests that the Lord was in the separation. Also, the naming of Joseph's second son, Ephraim, meaning "double fruit," suggests that Joseph felt fruitful in the land of sorrow. The separation from his family may have caused him to face the dysfunction of his youth.

PATTERNS OF HEALTH

Our culture needs transitional people. Many of us will have to go through twelve-step programs to be totally freed from abusive patterns that have shaped us.

The figure of Gideon represents how the power of the Holy Spirit heals the idolatry of our youth (see Judg. 6). Immediately after receiving his call to be a deliverer of Israel, Gideon is instructed to destroy all the false idols in his father's grove. This caused quite a stir in his town. In fact, his father had to intervene so that the villagers wouldn't kill him.

What is the Holy Spirit trying to teach us in this account? We all must destroy the idols of our youth and take seriously the dysfunctional patterns that will disrupt our dreams of fulfillment. The Holy Spirit wants us to appreciate and love our families while receiving His perfect Fatherhood in our lives.

TRANSITIONAL PEOPLE CELEBRATED

Several years ago I coauthored a book with an evangelist named Ron Rearick. Ron spent twenty of his first thirty years incarcerated. (That included many years as a juvenile delinquent!) He was once arrested for attempting to take $1 million from United Airlines through a hijack threat.

I was fascinated with his story. I was also disturbed by the cruelty he had seen in his life. He acquired the name Iceman after he popped an eye right out of the skull of a would-be rapist in prison. He was a tough guy. Now he was gentle.

"Ron, how did you get so hard and mean?" I asked him.

Ron leaned back in his chair, a bit choked up. "I know exactly how it happened. My father was an alcoholic. We moved from mining town to mining town — wherever he could find work in his trade as an engineer. He was never sober enough to take me fishing or do any of the other things the other kids did, so I would make up lies. I would tell the kids how we went fishing, how many fish we caught, and so on. As I told these lies, I became more and more angry with my father for putting me in that position."

"When did you recognize that this was an issue, and how did you turn it around?" I asked.

Ron, wiping his eyes, continued, "One morning, standing and looking at myself in a mirror, I realized I had to get rid of this hate I had for my father. As soon as I asked God to help me forgive him, I saw him as a child. I realized that he treated me exactly the way he had been treated. Inside he was a little child who had never grown up. If I was to grow in the Lord, it was time to face that and grow up myself."

"So what steps did you take?" I asked, intrigued.

"I did two things, Doug. I forgave my father, and I received God as my Father. I felt immediately restored and healed inside."

I believe that Ron became a transitional figure in his family. Now he also reaches hundreds of kids for Christ each year. He lives in a prison town near us, ministering to and visiting other prisoners' families. He knows the power of being a transitional person.

ANOTHER TRANSITION

Sue could be any number of people I have known who have been manic-depressive. This kind of depression is genetic. The general population knows so little about it in our culture, yet it is very prevalent. Effective treatments have been developed.

Sue's family had struggled for several generations with the manic-depressive disease. Some of the symptoms were not sleeping, marital conflict and an inability to stay focused on goals. Depression can be misunderstood because it looks like a moral or spiritual issue. "After all, how do Christians not have joy if they are truly saved?" we ask.

Sue finally found help in an encounter group. She was introduced to a psychiatrist in our community who treated her with antidepressants and counseled her as to the genetic nature of the depression. She began to realize that the depression had filled both sides of her family and talked openly about her healing. She had found joy by getting proper chemical balance. She was able to experience pleasure again and set goals for her life. The result has been an awareness that has grown multigenerationally in her family.

Another hero I have known we will call Jane. She is now a counselor for addicts. For multiple generations her family members had all been alcoholic. "If you were a Jones," she said, "you were an alcoholic. That was just the way it was."

After two broken marriages and broken health, Jane

decided that the pattern had to be broken. Her son and daughter were both alcoholics and drug addicts. Her elderly parents were still caught in the grips of addiction. "That's enough," she said.

Not only did she give her heart to Christ, but she went through a twelve-step program. She learned the nature of addiction and how it works genetically, and she was able to overcome the disease of alcoholism that had ravaged her family for generations.

The result of her courage to speak out was that dreams were restored to her family. Her son became drug-free and gave his heart to Christ, as did her daughter.

Jane, Sue and Ron are all modern-day Josephs. Their dreams were restored to them by overcoming the dysfunction of their families. Our culture needs transitional persons.

TRANSITIONAL CHURCHES

Not only do we need transitional persons, but we also need transitional churches. Unfortunately, lack of knowledge sometimes makes churches resistant. One church in our community discontinued a support group for depressed people because the group leaders encouraged the people to take the medication their doctors prescribed for their depression. This church obviously did not understand the true nature of some of these genetic and physical disorders.

Does this mean that God cannot heal these people without medication? I don't believe that. But I believe we need to be willing to accept medical treatment for mental health just as much as we are willing to accept medical treatment for a broken leg. In either case, we need to let the Lord tell us whether He wants to accomplish healing without medical treatment.

TRANSITIONAL DREAMERS

Joseph set the stage for a changed nation of Israel to emerge out of Egypt several centuries after it arrived. He was the transition from the people of Israel being a renegade band of dysfunctional, deceitful nomads to being God's chosen nation. They would be the people from whom the Messiah, the Savior of the world, would come.

Our own nation is adrift in dysfunction just as Joseph's people were. Even our churches are often toxic. Dreamers are being raised up for "such a time as this" (Esth. 4:14). Our challenge is to say enough is enough and move the nation into a new season of health. The gentle call of those who have been healed from scars of dysfunction in their own lives will lead the way.

I think another way to describe transitional persons or groups is to say they are people affected by revival. A revival is a transition from spiritual sickness to spiritual health. A revival from God can be a spiritual transition for an entire generation.

LIFE APPLICATION

- Do you recognize dysfunctions from your family of origin that may be affecting the release of your dreams?

- Are you willing to make clear and steadfast steps to remedy the impact on your own life and be healed?

- Have you been victimized by the dysfunctions of others?

- Are you available to the Holy Spirit to be a stage-setter for the outbreaking of His power in your community?

A transitional person's pain becomes the doorway to

healing for others. The best person to help a depressed person is someone who has faced and overcome depression themselves. An addict or an alcoholic is most likely to listen to someone who himself has been healed and restored.

The discovery of your dreams may reside at the point of your greatest pain. By running and hiding from your pain, you may be running from your greatest dream.

A member of my congregation handed me the following parable (author unknown). It illustrates the agony of the process of transition and the joy that follows.

PARABLE OF THE TWINS

Once upon a time, twin boys were conceived in the same womb. Weeks passed, and the twins developed. As their awareness grew, they laughed for joy: "Isn't it great that we were conceived? Isn't it great to be alive?"

Together, the twins explored their world. When they found their mother's cord that gave them life, they sang for joy: "How great is our mother's love, that she shares her own life with us!"

As weeks stretched into months, the twins noticed how much each was changing. "What does it mean?" asked the one.

"It means that our stay in this world is drawing to an end," said the other.

"But I don't want to go," the first replied. "I want to stay here always."

"We have no choice," said the other, "but maybe there is life after birth!"

"But how can there be?" responded the one. "We will shed our life cord, and how is life possible without it? Besides, we have seen evidence that others were here before us, and none of them has returned to tell us that there is life after birth. No, this is the end."

And so the one fell into deep despair, saying, "If conception ends in birth, what is the purpose of life in the womb? It's meaningless! Maybe there is not a mother after all."

"But there has to be," protested the other. "How else did we get here? How do we remain alive?"

"Have you ever seen our mother?" said the one. "Maybe she lives only in our minds. Maybe we made her up because the idea made us feel good."

And so the last days in the womb were filled with deep questioning and fear. Finally the moment of birth arrived.

When the twins had passed from their world, they opened their eyes. They cried. For what they saw exceeded their fondest dreams.

No eye has seen, no ear has heard,
no mind has conceived what God has prepared
for those who love him (1 Cor. 2:9).

FOURTEEN

BLESSING DREAMERS

All these are the twelve tribes of Israel, and this
is what their father said to them when he
blessed them, giving each the blessing appropriate to him (Gen. 49:28).

The blessing in a Hebrew family was more than just a
nice social exercise. It was believed to have tangible ef-
fects on the future. The pronouncement of a blessing from
the patriarch assured victory, success and fulfillment of
one's dreams. Even Joseph, who spent years separated
from his family, longed for the blessing of his father to
achieve the dreams God had for him.

Every dreamer needs a blesser.

In the New Testament a blessing is equivalent to the gift of encouragement. In the book of Acts, Barnabas was called the "son of encouragement" because he was always encouraging the work of the Lord (Acts 4:36-37). He was a blesser. He sold land and gave the money to the apostles to finance the work of the Lord.

The art of blessing does not need to be lost in our time. Blessing can be given in three dimensions:

- Presence

- Word

- Touch

THE BLESSING OF PRESENCE

My grandfather was retired from construction work quite a long while by the time I hit high school. Yet he would appear on the site of numerous jobs that my uncles were carrying on in their construction company. I was usually a supply carrier for the company during summer breaks. I can remember how I looked forward to my grandfather appearing on the jobs. He would always have a comment on how the job was progressing — sometimes to the annoyance of my uncles. At other times not.

But his presence on the site was always a blessing.

I couldn't count the number of times that grown men have shared with me, "My father was never there for my concert or my ball game or my graduation." There is a blessing of presence that is essential if we are to believe we're supported. Just being there sometimes is enough of a blessing to raise courage and dispel fears.

I recently rushed to the hospital to visit a terminally ill patient. I really didn't know what to say. When I walked into the room, this close friend extended her hand for me to take. I gently began to speak a few words of hope. Then we just sat there, with two of our other friends, in silence.

She would die two days later. None of us in the room knew how near she was to death.

After a time the room became uncomfortably quiet. "Judy," I began, "I don't know what to say except that I just feel like I'm supposed to be here. Whether it's a blessing or not, I don't know. But I'm here."

She smiled and responded, "Just being here is more than enough. It's building my faith as you just sit there."

THE BLESSING OF WORDS

A kind word cheers (Prov. 12:25).

The tongue that brings healing is a tree of life (Prov. 15:4).

Pleasant words are...sweet to the soul and healing to the bones (Prov. 16:24).

A word aptly spoken is like apples of gold in settings of silver (Prov. 25:11).

Of all the teachers I had in school, I remember one in particular. Her name was Mrs. Beatty. She wasn't a disciplinarian. And if we got right down to it, I didn't learn much math or geography from her either.

But I'll never forget the day in third grade when she read a two-paragraph short story I had written. I don't recall ever having exceptional ideas. And I really didn't stand out much, particularly in grade school. Yet, after reading it, she looked at me and said, "Doug, you are a very creative person. I think you could do well at being a writer."

I stored those words in my heart. Years later when I was asked to write a column, I saw the image of Mrs. Beatty over my desk, saying, "You're very creative, Doug. I think you could be a writer." I found courage in her words twenty years later.

This is the power of the blessing of words.

The first time I prophesied was a memorable event. I had never been exposed to spiritual gifts. When I came to the Lord, I attended every kind of meeting possible. I got involved in the most radical, charismatic, Pentecostal services you could imagine. It was there I observed people prophesying.

Upon returning from a charismatic conference to our home church, I felt that I had a prophecy. Now the room was small enough — it seated about two hundred people — that a prophecy given at a volume two on a scale of one to ten would have been sufficient.

But I got so excited I screamed out the prophecy. My parents were there, and I nearly scared them to death. (They hadn't fully committed their lives to the Lord yet.) I even hyperventilated and had to sit down in the chair. It shook everybody up. The service came to a screeching halt. No one could interpret or understand what I said because I had done such a poor job of sharing it.

The pastor very gently instructed the congregation that it was OK, that it was a legitimate word from the Lord, but it had been given in a way that obstructed the service.

As soon as the service was over, an elderly gentleman in the congregation sat me down and put his arm around my shoulders. "You know, I had the same prophecy," he said. "And do you know it's in the Bible? Here, let me show you the verse." He pointed out that I'd actually quoted a section of the book of Isaiah verbatim — though I had never read it before in my life.

"You're good at this," he said. "I'll bet Pastor Larry would like to talk to you about it." I went up to the front of the auditorium to apologize for causing such a disruption. By now it had sunk into me that I hadn't given it quite right.

As I walked into the prayer room, he began to laugh.

"Doug, it was a great word. You just did a terrible job of giving it. You see, what you did wrong is that you drew attention to yourself. The words of the Lord are to bring attention to the Lord. So you find a way to give His words so that people think of Him more than they think of you. By the way, you need to do that again. The next time you receive a prophecy, I want you to share it, because you're good at it."

With that encouragement my fear of the supernatural was abated. I felt blessed. Words had blessed and encouraged a dream.

History records the lives of two young men who shared the experience of dropping a carafe of communion wine. The first, in a small village of Yugoslavia, dropped the blessed carafe on the floor of a small parish. Consecrated wine spilled every which way as it shattered. The priest in a fit of anger commanded the young altar boy to leave the church and never return again. If he was not going to take the things of God more seriously, the priest said, he wasn't welcome.

The other young man who dropped a carafe was in a large cathedral in the presence of Bishop John Spalding. As an elderly man he would recall the volume of this carafe as it hit the cathedral floor, with its crash echoing through the giant vaults above. "It was like an atomic bomb going off in my head," he would say. This young man looked up into the eyes of the bishop, expecting to be chastised. Instead the bishop said, "You're a fine young man. Someday you're going to be doing what I'm doing."

The first young man became the atheist head of the Communist party in Yugoslavia. We know him as Tito. The second boy became one of the first television preachers — and a very successful one at that — Archbishop Fulton Sheen.

The blessing of words can set the course of an entire life.

I've had a growing desire in my heart to bless people

with words. I look for opportunities to write notes or cards for people, encouraging their dreams. I just want to say, "Dream on!"

Just a few words from my friend Jamie Buckingham were comforting to me at one point in my life. He had flown to Seattle to visit us after hearing we had left a staff position to start a new congregation on the east side of Seattle with no people, no money, nothing. He looked at me honestly and said, "I think you're crazy. But if you're going to start a new congregation, I want to be part of it. So count me in. I want to be part of this dream."

The exciting part was that Jamie made good on his promise by speaking in our church on a yearly basis for about ten years. He encouraged our dreams and cheered us on. People in our congregation don't know what be-hind-the-scenes blessers he and his wife, Jackie, both were.

Every dream needs a blesser.

THE BLESSING OF TOUCH

The blessing of touch includes:

- Physical touch.

- Making contact with another person's life.

The Scriptures show that dreams are often set in mo-tion by the laying on of hands. In the book of Acts, Barnabas and Paul were set apart for a special ministry by a prophecy. But that wasn't enough to release the dream. The Bible says the members of the church "placed their hands on them and sent them off" (Acts 13:1-3).

Beyond that, the power of touch lies in a willingness to become engaged in another person's life, to invest in their dreams. Have you touched anyone else's dreams lately? Have you sent them a gift or extended some tangible expression of involvement? On the other hand, have you thanked the people who have deliberately invested in your dream?

Few dreams have grown out of chastisement. Multitudes have become dreamers through encouragement. One of the primary points of blessing should be the home.

At the end of Genesis we read about a moving scene where Joseph and his brothers are gathered to hear the final words from their father, Jacob. I picture a weathered, wise man reverently extending his hands to each of his sons, leaving a touch he knew would be with them forever.

LIFE APPLICATION

- Can you recognize those whom the Lord has used to bless your dream? Have you expressed gratitude to them?

- If you haven't already, would you accept an assignment to make a deliberate list of people whose dreams you would bless?

FIFTEEN

THE LEGACY

And Joseph made the sons of Israel swear an oath and said, "God will surely come to your aid, and then you must carry my bones up from this place" (Gen. 50:25).

Now Joseph and all his brothers and all that generation died, but the Israelites were fruitful and multiplied greatly and became exceedingly numerous, so that the land was filled with them (Ex. 1:6-7).

Have you ever noticed that certain people are like large boats on a lake? You know, you are sitting in your little rowboat, and some boat comes by with two power motors on the back, leaving a wake that makes your boat rock and roll on the tumble of the waves. People like this are "wave-makers." This is what biblical dreamers are like. Each one leaves a legacy, like ripples following a boat.

It sounds great to leave a legacy, doesn't it? But the flip side of that means that the fulfillment of your dreams may not happen until after you are gone. True dreams of God can take longer than one life to be fulfilled. Sometimes they take longer than a lifetime even to come into view.

This concept challenges some of our eschatology, or views of the end times. After all, how much time can we count on before the Lord brings this age to a close? Do we have hundreds of years to plan for, or will it all be over before our time comes to die?

I have studied the questions enough to conclude that I am rather unclear about most points of eschatology. It is clear to me, however, that our opinions about the future will shape our actions today. I have concluded that we ought to be prepared for the end to come at any moment, yet we ought to go on investing as though the Lord may not come for five hundred years.

DREAMERS SEE BEYOND THE END

In Stephen R. Covey's book *The Seven Habits of Highly Effective People*, he suggests that one of the habits of highly effective people is starting from the end and working backward. In fact, this is the difference between efficient and inefficient people. Effective people can see a completed task and work toward it. The ability to visualize to the end is vital to success.[1]

If you have ever been a leader of people, you've realized what a rare skill this is. No doubt you have also discovered your own deficiencies. It is amazing how prone we are not to know where we are headed.

Here is an exciting insight about dreamers. Dreamers look several generations ahead and then live backward.

I enjoy hanging out with businesspeople. I think Christianity works best in the marketplace. Businesspeople often have clearer spiritual insights than people who work full-time for churches.

I like to eavesdrop on businesspeople's conversations. On one of these occasions I heard two men talking about how they were planning for their business. One commented, "You know, I read recently that a company in Japan has a 250-year plan." (I thought, Wow! 250 years!)

"Can you imagine?" the other shook his head and laughed. "If I could get my team to look ahead three months I'd be satisfied."

"Maybe that's why the Japanese are beating us," the first one concluded. "When multiple generations combine to see a dream fulfilled, there is a lot more oomph behind it."

LEAVING A LEGACY

Joseph's life ends with a description of the legacy he left. For generations the impact of his life rippled on through family after family in the wake of the discovery that God was very much alive in developing a nation.

In his book *Who Switched the Price Tags?*, Tony Campolo refers to a study compiled from a sampling of near centenarians.

> Recently I read a sociological study that has great significance for those of us who are trying to respond to champions of the yuppie value system. In this particular study fifty people over the age of ninety-five were asked one question: "If you could live your life over again what would you do differently?" It was an open-ended question, and these elderly people were allowed to

respond in unstructured ways. As you might imagine, a multiplicity of answers came from these eldest of senior citizens. However, three answers constantly re-emerged and dominated the results of the study. These three answers were: 1) if I had to do it over again, I would reflect more; 2) if I had to do it over again, I would risk more; 3) if I had to do it over again, I would do more things that would live on after I am dead.[2]

How many things are you involved in that will outlive your life?

What about your dream? Will it outlast you? Sit down with a piece of paper, and write out at least ten of them. I have. It is an exciting prospect. I think you will be pleasantly surprised about how many things the Lord has allowed you to be involved in that will go on beyond you.

On the other hand, we really cannot know for certain what things will outlast our lives. That is where trusting the Holy Spirit comes in. We can pray, "Holy Spirit, lead me in ways today that will make an impact beyond my life span."

PREPARE THE WAY

Every generation needs a previous generation to prepare the way for them to dream. Dreamers don't consume all of tomorrow's resources today. Dreamers save up portions of today's resources to fuel the part of their dream that will go beyond them. In our generationally disrupted culture, this is a difficult concept to grasp.

As a leader of a congregation focusing on baby boomers, I have been concerned at how we boomers are so cut off from our futures. I am just as concerned about the way the previous generation profitted off the sheer size of the boomer generation. Housing costs rose astronomically, and previous generations profitted greatly while many boomers were not able to have the same future their parents had.

The problem has been spiritual as well. A strong work of God requires the combined harmony of multiple generations. Satan performed a damaging work in the 1960s by dividing fathers from sons, mothers from daughters. But the gulf between these two generations is not too large for God.

My heart broke the other day when I heard a news commentator say that scholars are concluding that the present inner-city generation of teens ought to be abandoned. This whole generation of young black men should be written off, according to the black commentator. He believed we should begin working on those who are five and younger. It is hoped that our cities will have a future. God gives up on no generation.

I believe this is what happens when there is shortsighted profiteering at any level of a society. I am trying to lead our congregation with these questions in mind:

- What are we going to do that will help set the stage for the next generation?

- How are we going to reserve funds for the future?

- How can our facilities outlast us sufficiently to be used again?

- How can I keep my heart tender and sensitive enough so that when the methods need to be changed, I will trust the younger generation to carry on?

Dreamers are flexible. Dreamers look to the future. Dreamers invest beyond themselves.

MENTORS, STEP UP!

In the church, mentoring is a rare event. Yet education by information-dispensing has failed us. Education by modeling is proving to be the way to develop leaders.

The biblical term for mentoring is *discipling*. Mentoring is simply a friend walking alongside a friend, helping that person to acquire skill and knowledge. As you mentor others, you are investing in a dream that can reach beyond your life.

A couple of years ago I was speaking at a friend's parish in the city of Spokane, about five hours from my home. I thoroughly enjoyed being with these people, but I was tired from the travel. I was ready to head home with the last amen. As I went to the side door, a young man and woman stepped up and said, "Can we talk to you a minute, Pastor Doug?" They were in their mid-twenties and seemed very excited to talk with me for a moment.

"Yes, how can I help you?" I asked, a little nervously.

"You probably don't recognize us," the husband said, "but we met Christ in your church several years ago."

"I was a high school student," the wife chimed in. "I gave my heart to the Lord, learned to worship and learned to love the Bible. Joe and I met in college, and we are in the ministry now. But we want to have a church just like Eastside. We just wanted you to know that. You may never hear from us or see us again, but the ripple of your life has touched ours."

I had never had an experience like that before. To think that I could impact someone enough that they would have made that kind of decision was overwhelming.

Sometimes we mentor and don't even know it. The young man confirmed this when he said further, "You taught me one thing."

"Oh, yes, what's that?" I asked.

"No matter what, just keep showing up," he said. "I know there were days when you were dog-tired, but you were still there."

His wife leaned forward to add, "We've told ourselves every day that we are just going to keep showing up."

Serious mentoring takes a deliberate choice to be yourself in front of others. It involves an investment of time in those who will follow us. It requires setting up models in churches and home groups where leaders learn to replace themselves.

None of us will be able to look Jesus squarely in the eye, whether we are a Sunday school teacher, a businessman for Christ, a publisher or a writer and expect Him to say, "Well done, good and faithful servant," unless we have answered these questions: Who will take my place, and how have I helped them?

CONFLICT OF THE GENERATIONS

We've talked about preparing for future generations and the value of mentoring. These two concepts are the key to resolving the conflict that keeps coming up between generations. What can be done? Let's look at three ideas.

- I think generations can work together if both younger and older learn to invest themselves in something bigger than themselves and the borders of their small worlds.

- To be a mentor requires honoring and respecting someone who has yet to make the same mistakes you made long ago.

- Dreams work best when children appreciate the heavy price parents or spiritual mentors have paid for some of the knowledge, resources and happiness the children take for granted.

Finally, we need to realize that God has a unique

dream for each generation. This is reinforced in Acts 13:36 when Paul commented, "David had served God's purpose in his own generation."

CREATIVE LEGACIES

We show videos of missionaries in our congregation from time to time. We find that being able to see an individual's face, while at the same time hearing from his or her heart, helps us put more feeling into the giving of dollars to missions.

Recently we viewed a brief video of one of our Foursquare missionaries in Nepal. He and his wife have adopted dozens of Nepalese children. The reason they have done this is that it is the only way they can evangelize. In Nepal it is illegal to proselytize for the Christian faith. However, one can evangelize his or her own family. Our missionary came up with a great strategy. He built an orphanage, which he calls his house, and began adopting as many children as he had the resources to feed.

His goal, as stated on the video, was to leave an entire younger generation that may be able to "evangelize in a time that is freer than his own." This statement struck my heart like a spear. He was deliberately laying a foundation in dozens and dozens of his children's lives, awaiting a day that he was praying for, a day when the gospel could be preached more freely.

What if some of our dreams are never fulfilled in our lifetime? How should we then live? Could it be that many of us are being called to walk by faith, not by sight, as we lay the foundations of our dreams? Could it be that we are being called to invest our lives for a time that will be more open and free to the gospel?

DOING THINGS THAT WILL LAST

My grandmother was one of the most wonderful people

you would ever want to meet. I'm not saying this just because she was my grandmother. Many others say the same thing.

My grandmother met Christ after the first sermon I preached. She was more than sixty-five years old, had cancer and had recently suffered a heart attack. She came forward during the altar call I gave. I thought she just wanted to encourage me. When I stepped down from the platform and asked her what she wanted, she said she wanted to "give her heart to Christ." She received Christ and lived more than ten years longer. She passed away in her sleep one afternoon in her living room.

My grandmother loved to make quilts. As she grew older, her fingers became arthritic, and it was very difficult to stitch the quilts that she made for every one of her grandchildren and great-grandchildren. It was her practice over several decades to make a quilt for each of her grandchildren when they were born and a larger one when they reached their early teens.

While I was visiting my grandmother one afternoon, I recall one of my aunts trying to talk her out of making any more quilts. The pain in my grandmother's fingers was intense. "I'll give you some money," my aunt said, "and you can simply buy the kids gifts this year. Mom, your hands are killing you. You don't need to do this."

"I want to leave them something that came from me," my grandmother responded. "I don't want to leave something you can buy. I want to leave a one-of-a-kind gift to my grandchildren. I want them, when they see this quilt, to see that I gave myself to them. I want them to hear me say, 'I love you,' even when I'm gone."

I have several of those quilts. One for each of my kids and one for my wife and me. The other night it was cold, and I pulled a quilt out of the closet and wrapped it around my feet. (It was a little worn by then.) Grandma was right. There was something of her in that room. She had invested herself in something that would outlast her.

And I appreciated her all over again that night. Leaving a legacy demands a piece of your heart left behind with others in mind.

SEATTLE'S FIRST PRESBYTERIAN CHURCH

Seattle is home to one of America's great churches. Two times I have stood in that church's hallways of honor and read its brief history. Later I was able to pick up a short newspaper article recounting the history of the First Presbyterian Church of Seattle.

The pastor of the First Presbyterian Church in Seattle for many years was a lawyer named Mark Matthews. Matthews and his congregation made it their aim to change the spiritual climate of the then-rugged city of Seattle. Out of the one congregation, several dozens of congregations were planted in Seattle, including University Presbyterian Church. Both churches have been home to noted pastors over the years.

When Matthews died, there was little or nothing in his estate. He had invested it all in his church. He left the church that he planted with a passion for our city that has continued to spread the gospel of Jesus Christ for multiple generations.

This church stands as a model to every church in every city.

So often we as believers get caught up in day-to-day affairs that sap the energy from our lives. How many congregations fight and quibble over the smallest of things without ever asking the question, What will we leave for future generations? Dreamers don't have time for petty affairs of the next ten minutes. Their assignments are too large for that.

Christians with dreams big enough to outlast themselves take giant risks. They also take time to consider what their futures may look like. Dreamers in a certain sense are Spirit-led "future creators."

HOPE THAT TRANSFORMS THE PRESENT

There is a paradigm shift from those who muddle around with their noses in the ground of daily affairs and those who lift their heads high to be visionaries for the future. Our character of focus, Joseph, was such a visionary. So was Daniel, the great prophet of the Old Testament.

Taken from his land of Judea as a teenager, he was held captive by the powerful government of Babylon. He had to redefine what it meant to be a Jew.

Daniel was able to make the transition from defining a Jew as someone who lived in Judea and worshipped in the temple in Jerusalem to someone who could serve the living God of Jerusalem anywhere, even in the city of Babylon.

He went one step further. He also began to prophesy of days when Israel would see her Messiah come in great power and subjugate all the great powers of the world. He remained faithful to God in a foreign land, laying the foundation for future generations. He and his friends would face any conflict in any fire to make certain there was a future for the Jewish people.

It was his legacy which became the remnant that returned to Jerusalem seventy years later. I don't think it is any accident that Daniel and Joseph were both the seers of dreams and interpreters of dreams in profound measures.

LIFE APPLICATION

- What have you spent your time on this week that will outlast you?

- Have you considered how you invest your financial resources in ways that will outlast you?

- Are you doing things that will make your time and yourself available for those who will live beyond you?

- Can you think of practical steps that both the church or your family can take to ensure a better future for your grandchildren?

SIXTEEN

CONCLUSION

We need to make a dramatic turn from being consumers to being investors. This will occur as we develop a dream and vision for the future. Our national indebtedness is obscene, but it reflects the kind of spirit that we are vulnerable to in our country: Eat, drink and be merry, for tomorrow we die.

In contrast Joseph challenges us to leave a legacy.

So you still want to be a dreamer? Do you recognize the theme of the symphony God is directing in your life? Joseph is our template for the various movements that can make up the symphony of our dreams. His life went through four major movements. Can you recognize at which movement you are in life?

- Movement one: mixed motives, unclear understanding of the dream, competitiveness, favoritism.

- Movement two: accused, suppressed, tempted, tested, forgotten.

- Movement three: opportunities to serve, seeing others' dreams fulfilled, humbly interpreting and applying the dreams of others while seeing yours unfulfilled.

- Movement four: maturity, fulfillment, forgiveness, leaving a legacy.

In a certain way, I think I am living in all four of these movements at once as I have examined my dreaming. As we come to the end of this book, I am certain that you have been made aware of the complexity of your own heart as well.

REVIEW

Let's review some of the vital principles we have gained on our journey through Joseph's life.

- You don't have God's dreams; they have you.

- There is a high cost to be paid for dreaming.

- There are dream seducers ready to throw you off course.

- Dreams thrive in the fertile ground of hostility.

- You are your dream's own worst enemy.

- Every dream has its blesser.

- Dreamers are transitional people leading others to wholeness and better days ahead.

- Your dreams should be big enough to outlast you.

THE BIG QUESTION

Have you ever just wanted to disappear? You know, pick up one day and go, never to be seen again? Have you ever wanted to return home as a hero, coming in as everyone's savior, saving the day? Of course, we all have.

I have wanted to disappear, from time to time, and see what people would say about me. In my daydreams I live across the street from my family, like the guy out of one of Nathaniel Hawthorne's stories. I would wear some sort of fake beard, maybe gain some extra weight, and then I could surreptitiously slip into conversations about me. I'd like to overhear what people say about me.

Why do we have thoughts like that? Like all dreamers, we want to make a difference. We want our lives to count. We want to be missed. Dreamers wonder what kind of void they would leave.

Let's return to our first four questions.

Rest assured, if you travel with Jesus, you will return home a hero! All dreamers do!

A COATLESS LORD

When the soldiers crucified Jesus, they took his clothes, dividing them into four shares, one for each of them, with the undergarment remaining. This garment was seamless, woven in one piece from top to bottom.

"Let's not tear it," they said to one another. "Let's decide by lot who will get it."

This happened that the scripture might be fulfilled which said, "They divided my garments among them and cast lots for my clothing" (John 19:23-24).

We can't forget there was more than one man in the Bible who lost His coat. His was a King's coat. He wore His coatlessness in great honor and deep love. The Roman soldiers first stripped Jesus of His humble coat and placed on Him a scarlet military cloak. He wore it with honor even in the face of their mocking. So they derobed Him again. Coatless, He was even more our Savior and more the King, beckoning this comment from one of the mocking Roman soldiers: "Surely this man was the Son of God!" (Mark 15:39).

Jesus knows what it's like to have a coat ripped off and keep His dreams. His dream was you. He knows how to help us keep our dreams when they steal our coats.

PRAYER

Lord, the pattern is set;
lead us on to dream in You,
for You and with You.
Amen.

APPENDIX A

OUTLINE OF JOSEPH'S LIFE

(SEE GEN. 37-50)

- The first son of Jacob's second and favorite wife, Rachel. He is the eleventh son in the family overall.
- At seventeen years old his father gives him a richly ornamented coat, a sign he would be the heir.
- At seventeen he has two dreams: one about sheaves of wheat bowing to him and one in which the stars, moon and sun bow to him. Joseph interprets this as his call to be the ruler of the family.
- He is hated by his brothers.
- His coat is taken away.
- He is tossed into a pit, sold into slavery to the Midianites and declared falsely dead to his father.
- One of Pharaoh's governors, Potiphar, buys Joseph.
- Potiphar's wife accuses him falsely of sexual harassment.
- He spends two years in prison.

- He interprets dreams for a baker and a cupbearer.

- The cupbearer forgets Joseph, who is left in prison.

- Joseph is released from prison to interpret the Pharaoh's two dreams — one dream showing seven healthy cows being swallowed up by seven starving cows, and the other showing seven good heads of grain eating seven withered heads of grain.

- He is appointed governor of the Egyptian crops at the age of thirty.

- His new name becomes Zaphenath-Paneah.

- He has two sons: Manasseh, whose name means "Elohim has made me forget the hardships and all my father's house," and Ephraim, whose name means "Elohim has made me fruitful in the land of my sorrows."

- His entire family, after three trips from Canaan, joins him in Goshen.

- His father, Jacob, dies, and he travels to Canaan to bury him.

- His relationship to his eleven brothers is restored.

- He dies at the age of 110.

APPENDIX B

JOSEPH'S FAMILY

This chart shows the mish-mash of a family that Joseph grew up in. Reading the chart from top to bottom shows the order of birth, starting with the oldest. Reading the chart from left to right shows the mothers of the twelve brothers and one sister in Joseph's immediate family.

MOTHERS:	Leah	Bilhah	Zilpah	Rachel
CHILDREN:				
	Reuben			
	Simeon			
	Levi			
	Judah			
		Dan		
		Naphtali		
			Gad	
			Asher	
	Issachar			
	Zebulun			
	Dinah			
				Joseph
				Benjamin

NOTES

CHAPTER 4

1. *Academic American Encyclopedia*, s.v. "dreams and dreaming." Grolier Electronic Publishing, Prodigy Service, December 19, 1992.

CHAPTER 5

1. Jennifer James, "A Mean Spirit Seems to Be Hampering Society's Growth," *Seattle Times*, 30 August 1992.

2. Madeleine L'Engle, *Sold Into Egypt: Joseph's Journey Into Human Being* (Wheaton, Ill.: Harold Shaw Publishers, 1989), p. 22.

3. Stephen R. Covey, *Principle-Centered Leadership* (New York: Summit Books, 1991).

CHAPTER 7

1. Jamie Buckingham, *Where Eagles Soar* (Lincoln, Va.: Chosen Books, 1980).

CHAPTER 11

1. William T. McConnell, *The Gift of Time* (Downers Grove, Ill.: InterVarsity Press, 1983), p. 19.

2. Quoted in Bob Benson Sr. and Michael W. Benson, *Disciplines for the Inner Life* (Nashville, Tenn.: Gener-

oux/Nelson, 1989), p. 182.

CHAPTER 12

1. *Ibid.*, p. 211.

CHAPTER 13

1. Wendy Kaminer, *I'm Dysfunctional, You're Dysfunctional* (Reading, Mass.: Addison-Wesley Publishing Co., 1992).
2. Cherry Boone O'Neill and Dan O'Neill, *Living on the Border of Disorder* (Minneapolis, Minn.: Bethany House, 1992).

CHAPTER 15

1. Stephen R. Covey, *The Seven Habits of Highly Effective People* (New York: Simon & Schuster Trade, 1989).
2. Anthony Campolo, *Who Switched the Price Tags?* (Irving, Tex.: Word, 1987).

BIBLIOGRAPHY

Benson, Bob, Sr., and Michael W. Benson. *Disciplines for the Inner Life*. Nashville, Tenn.: Generoux/Nelson, 1989.

Buckingham, Jamie. *Where Eagles Soar*. Lincoln, Va.: Chosen Books, 1980.

Campolo, Anthony. *Who Switched the Price Tags?* Irving, Tex.: Word, 1987.

Covey, Stephen R. *Principle-Centered Leadership*. New York: Summit Books, 1991.

————. *The Seven Habits of Highly Effective People*. New York: Simon & Schuster Trade, 1989.

Crabb, Larry, and Dan Allender. *Encouragement: The Key to Caring*. Grand Rapids, Mich.: Zondervan Publishing, 1984.

Dolnick, Edward. "What Dreams Are (Really) Made Of." *The Atlantic*, July 1990.

Gutheil, Emil. *Handbook of Dream Analysis*. New York: Liveright Publishing, 1951.

Hirsch, S. Carl. *Theater of the Night: What We Do and Do Not Know About Dreams*. Chicago: Rand McNally & Co., 1976.

James, Jennifer. "A Mean Spirit Seems to Be Hampering Society's Growth." Seattle, Wash.: *Seattle Times*, 30 August 1992.

Kaminer, Wendy. *I'm Dysfunctional, You're Dysfunctional*. Reading, Mass.: Addison-Wesley Publishing Co., 1992.

Lewis, C. S. *The Problem of Pain*. New \
Publishing Co., 1962.

L'Engle, Madeleine. *Sold Into Egypt: Josep
Into Human Being*. Wheaton, Ill.: Harold Ŝ.
lishers, 1989.

MacKenzie, Norman. *Dreams and Dreaming*. New York:
The Vanguard Press, 1965.

Manning, Brennan. *The Ragamuffin Gospel: Good News
for the Bedraggled, Beat-Up, and Burnt-Out*. Portland,
Oreg.: Multnomah Press, 1990.

McConnell, James V. *Understanding Human Behavior*.
New York: Harcourt, Brace, Jovanovich College Publishers, 1989.

McConnell, William T. *The Gift of Time*. Downers Grove,
Ill.: InterVarsity Press, 1983.

Meyer, F. B. *Old Testament Men of Faith*. Westchester,
Ill.: Good News Publishers, 1979.

Miller, Calvin. *The Table of Inwardness*. Downers Grove,
Ill.: InterVarsity Press, 1984.

Nouwen, Henri J. *Lifesigns, Intimacy, Fecundity, and Ec-
stasy in Christian Perspective*. New York: Doubleday &
Co., 1986.

O'Neill, Cherry Boone, and Dan O'Neill. *Living on the Border of Disorder: How to Cope With an Addictive Person*.
Minneapolis, Minn.: Bethany Publishing House, 1992.

Riffel, Herman. *Your Dreams: God's Neglected Gift*. Lincoln, Va.: Chosen Books, 1981.

Sanford, John A. *Dreams: God's Forgotten Language*.
Philadelphia: J. B. Lippincott Co., 1968.

Stigers, Harold G. *A Commentary on Genesis*. Grand Rapids, Mich.: Zondervan Publishing, 1976.

Strong, Polly. *Thirteen Authorities Tell You What Your
Dreams Mean*. New York: Berkley Publishing Group,
1990.

Tenney, Merrill C. *The Zondervan Pictorial Encyclopedia
of the Bible*, vols. II & V. Grand Rapids, Mich.: Zondervan Publishing, 1975.

If you enjoyed *Keeping Your Dreams Alive When They Steal Your Coat* we would like to recommend the following books:

Beyond Your Own Strength
by Frank Damazio
Don't let circumstances, problems, your past
or the opinions and criticisms of others defeat you.
Author Frank Damazio encourages you to go beyond your
limitations and become all that God wants you to be.

Being Happy in an Unhappy World
by John Hagee
John Hagee writes that money, pleasure and other
false formulas do not bring happiness. Jesus gave us the
foolproof formula for happiness in the eight beatitudes.

Hanging by a Thread
by Mark Rutland
The future of civilization hangs by a thread — the thread
of virtue. Without condemning, Mark Rutland challenges
Christians to reevaluate their life-styles.

Barefoot to the White House
by Carolyn Sundseth with Jimi Miller
Called to work in the White House when she was a
barefoot grandmother in Hawaii, Carolyn Sundseth,
with Jimi Miller, humorously tells how God used
her weaknesses to accomplish great works.

Available at your local Christian bookstore or from:

Creation House
600 Rinehart Road
Lake Mary, FL 32746
1-800-451-4598